D.I.Y. DENTISTRY

ANDY RILEY IS THE AUTHOR/ARTIST OF
*THE BOOK OF BUNNY SUICIDES, RETURN OF
THE BUNNY SUICIDES, GREAT LIES TO
TELL SMALL KIDS, LOADS MORE LIES
TO TELL SMALL KIDS, AND BUNNY
SUICIDES POSTCARD BOOK.* HIS WEEKLY
STRIP, *ROASTED*, RUNS IN THE OBSERVER
MAGAZINE.

HIS SCRIPTWRITING WORK INCLUDES
*BLACK BOOKS, LITTLE BRITAIN,
SLACKER CATS, HYPERDRIVE, SMACK
THE PONY, BIG TRAIN, THE ARMANDO
IANNUCCI SHOWS, SPITTING IMAGE,
SO GRAHAM NORTON, THE 99p CHALLENGE*
AND THE BAFTA-WINNING ANIMATION
ROBBIE THE REINDEER.

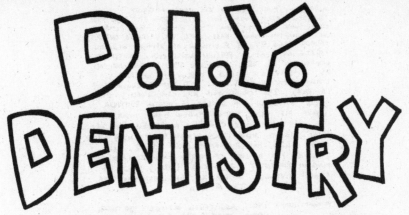

D.I.Y. DENTISTRY

...AND OTHER ALARMING INVENTIONS

ANDY RILEY

A PLUME BOOK

PLUME — PUBLISHED BY THE PENGUIN GROUP
PENGUIN GROUP (USA.) INC., 375 HUDSON ST., NEW YORK,
NEW YORK 10014, USA ⟣ PENGUIN GROUP (CANADA)
90 EGLINGTON AVENUE EAST, SUITE 700, TORONTO, ONTARIO,
CANADA M4P 2Y3 (A DIVISION OF PEARSON PENGUIN
CANADA INC.) ⟣ PENGUIN BOOKS LTD., 80 STRAND,
LONDON WC2R ORL, ENGLAND ⟣ PENGUIN IRELAND,
25 ST. STEPHEN'S GREEN, DUBLIN 2, IRELAND (A
DIVISION OF PENGUIN BOOKS LTD.) ⟣ PENGUIN GROUP
(AUSTRALIA), 250 CAMBERWELL RD, CAMBERWELL, VICTORIA
3124, AUSTRALIA (A DIVISION OF PEARSON AUSTRALIA
GROUP PTY. LTD.) ⟣ PENGUIN BOOKS INDIA PVT.
LTD., 11 COMMUNITY CENTRE, PANCHSHEEL PARK, NEW
DELHI - 110017, INDIA ⟣ PENGUIN GROUP (NZ), 67
APOLLO DRIVE, ROSEDALE, NORTH SHORE 0632, NEW
ZEALAND (A DIVISION OF PEARSON NEW ZEALAND LTD.)
PENGUIN BOOKS (SOUTH AFRICA) (PTY.) LTD., 24
STURDEE AVENUE, ROSEBANK, JOHANNESBURG, 2196,
SOUTH AFRICA

PENGUIN BOOKS LTD., REGISTERED OFFICES : 80 STRAND,
LONDON WC2 ORL, ENGLAND

PUBLISHED BY PLUME, A MEMBER OF PENGUIN GROUP (USA)
INC. — THIS IS AN AUTHORIZED REPRINT OF A HARDCOVER
EDITION PUBLISHED BY HODDER & STOUGHTON. FOR INFORMATION,
ADDRESS : HODDER & STOUGHTON, 338 EUSTON ROAD, LONDON
NW1 3BH, ENGLAND.

FIRST PLUME PRINTING, APRIL 2009
10 9 8 7 6 5 4

CIP DATA IS AVAILABLE. ISBN 978-0-452-29003-7
PRINTED IN THE UNITED STATES OF AMERICA

BOOKS ARE AVAILABLE AT QUANTITY DISCOUNTS WHEN
USED TO PROMOTE PRODUCTS OR SERVICES. FOR
INFORMATION PLEASE WRITE TO: PREMIUM MARKETING
DIVISION, PENGUIN GROUP (USA) INC., 375 HUDSON ST.,
NEW YORK, NEW YORK 10014

WITH THANKS TO:

POLLY FABER, CAMILLA HORNBY,
BEN DUNN, ELENI FOSTIROPOULOS,
EVERYONE ELSE AT HODDER,
KEVIN CECIL, FELICITY BLUNT, FREYA AYRES

AND

W. HEATH ROBINSON
WILF LUNN

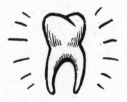

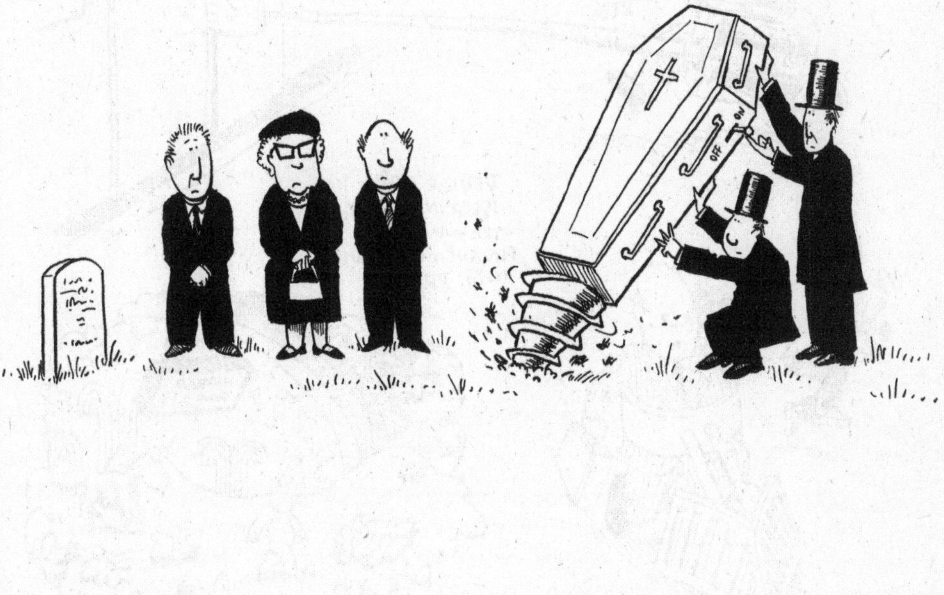
ON
OFF

SELF-BURYING COFFIN

IMPATIENT BUSINESSMAN

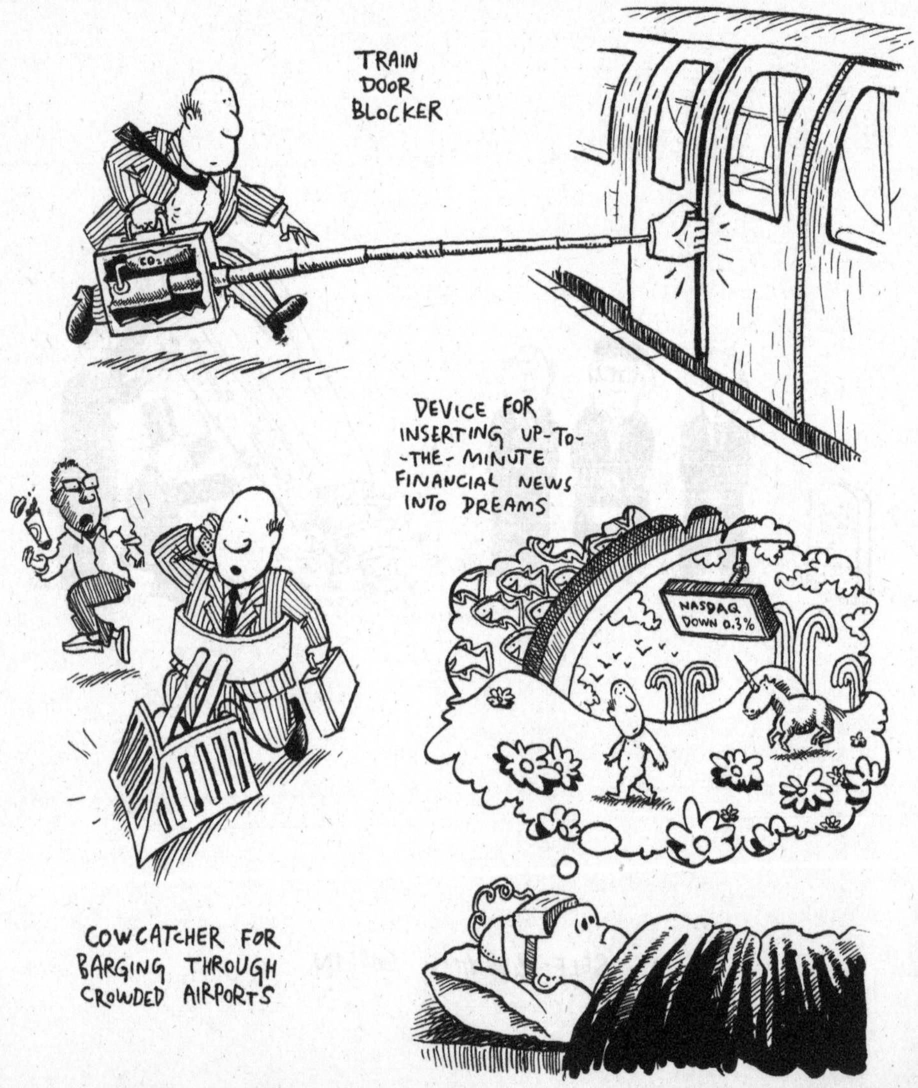

TRAIN DOOR BLOCKER
CO_2
DEVICE FOR INSERTING UP-TO--THE-MINUTE FINANCIAL NEWS INTO DREAMS
NASDAQ DOWN 0.3%
COWCATCHER FOR BARGING THROUGH CROWDED AIRPORTS

WORLD'S CHEAPEST HAIRDRYER

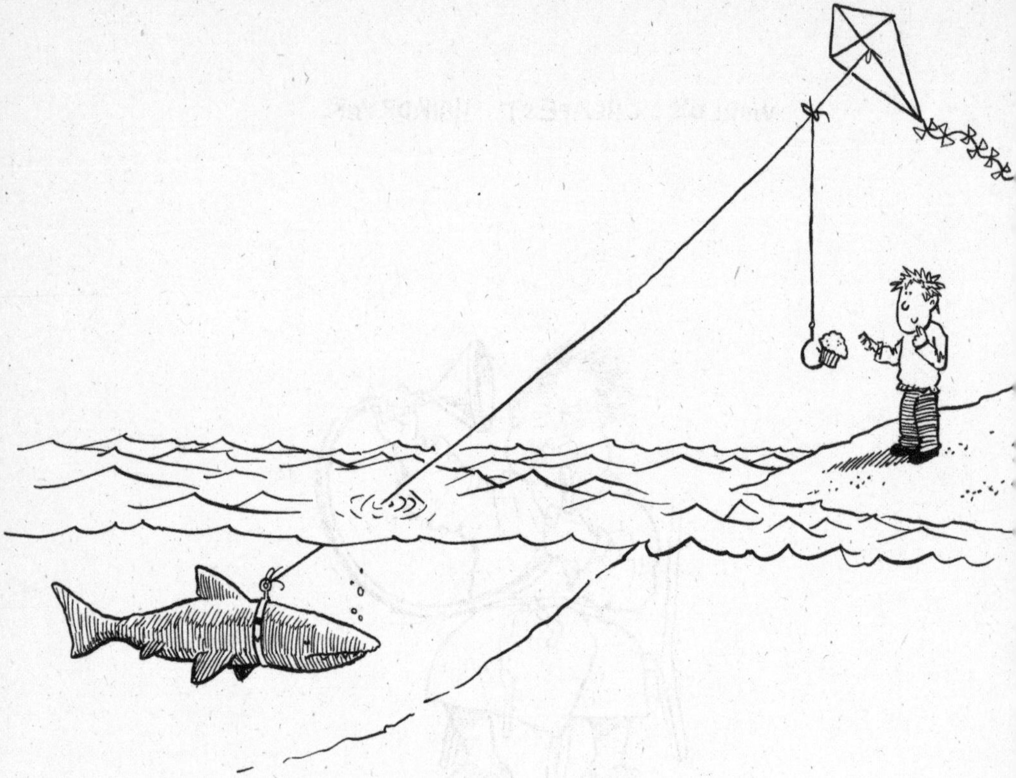

A METHOD FOR FISH
WHO WANT TO EVEN
THINGS UP A BIT

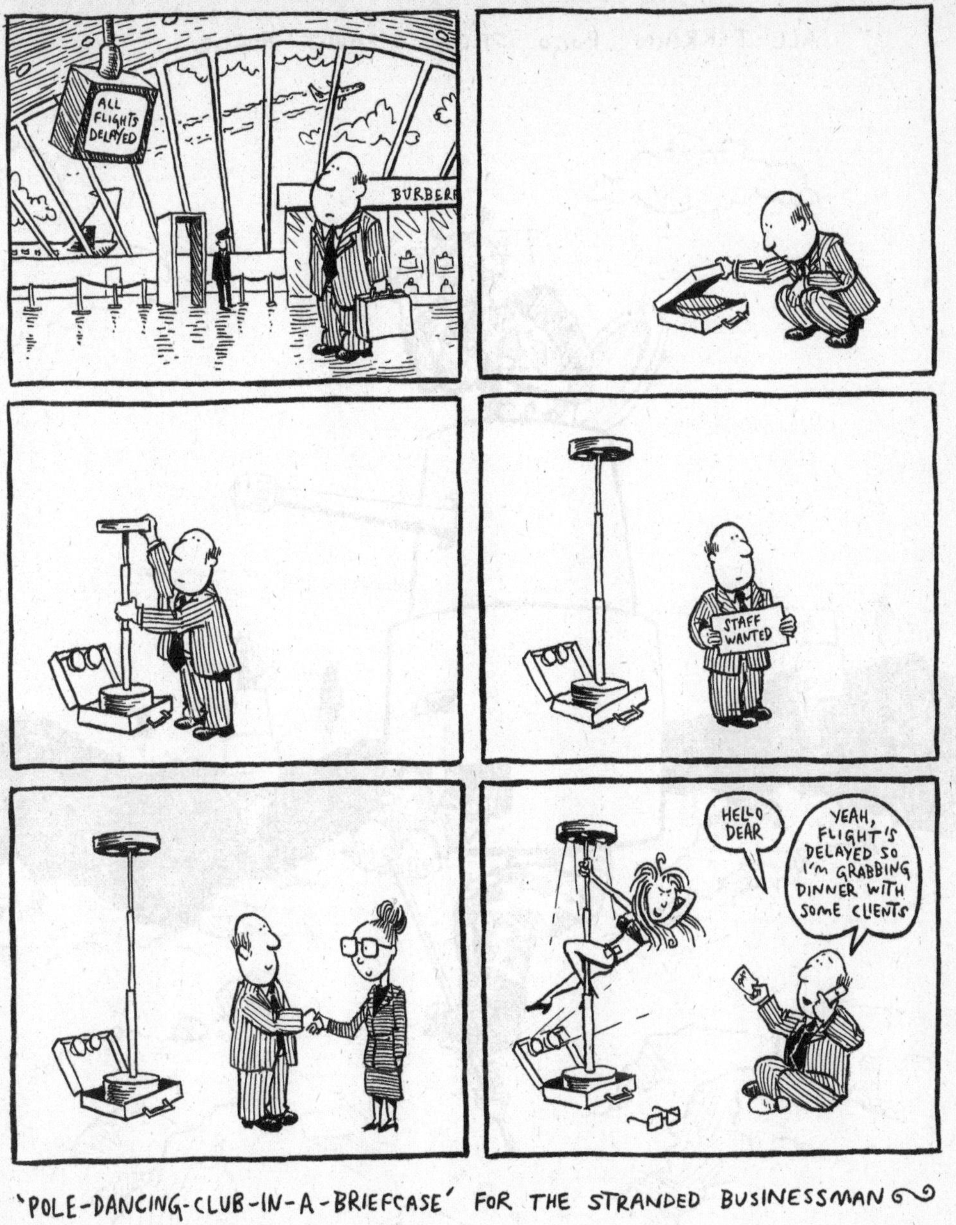
ALL FLIGHTS DELAYED
BURBERR
STAFF WANTED
HELLO DEAR
YEAH, FLIGHT'S DELAYED SO I'M GRABBING DINNER WITH SOME CLIENTS

'POLE-DANCING-CLUB-IN-A-BRIEFCASE' FOR THE STRANDED BUSINESSMAN

ALL-TERRAIN POGO STICK ASSAULT FORCE

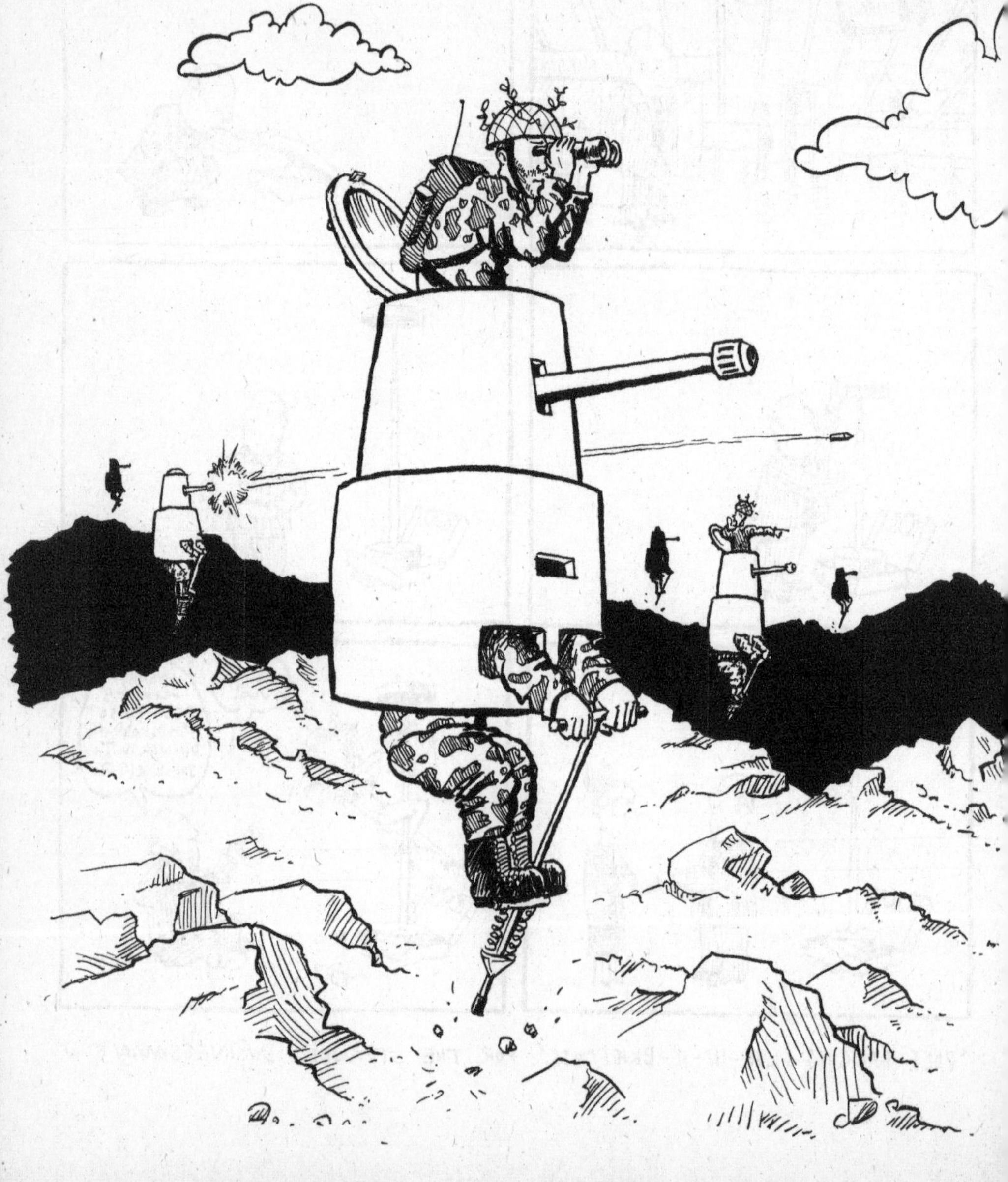

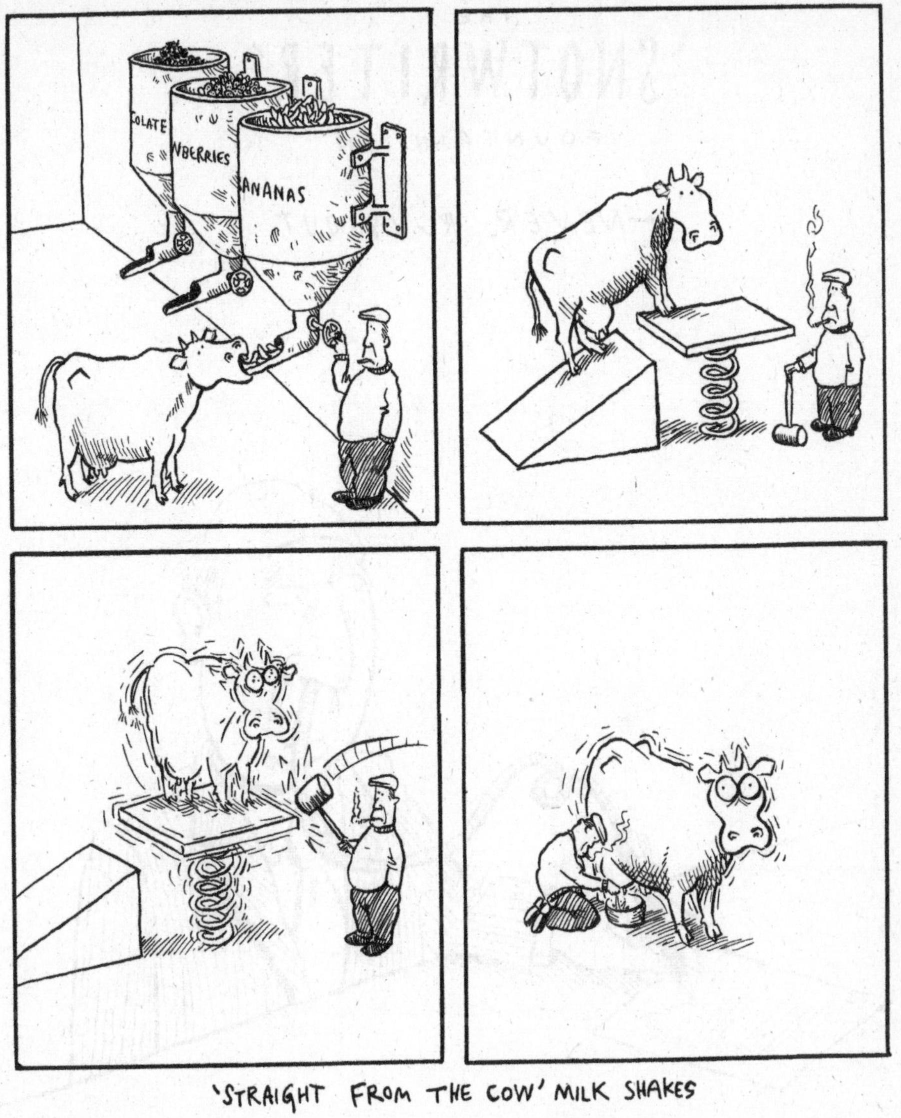
COLATE
WBERRIES
ANANAS

'STRAIGHT FROM THE COW' MILK SHAKES

THE

'SNOTWRITER'

FOUNTAIN PEN

—NEVER RUNS OUT

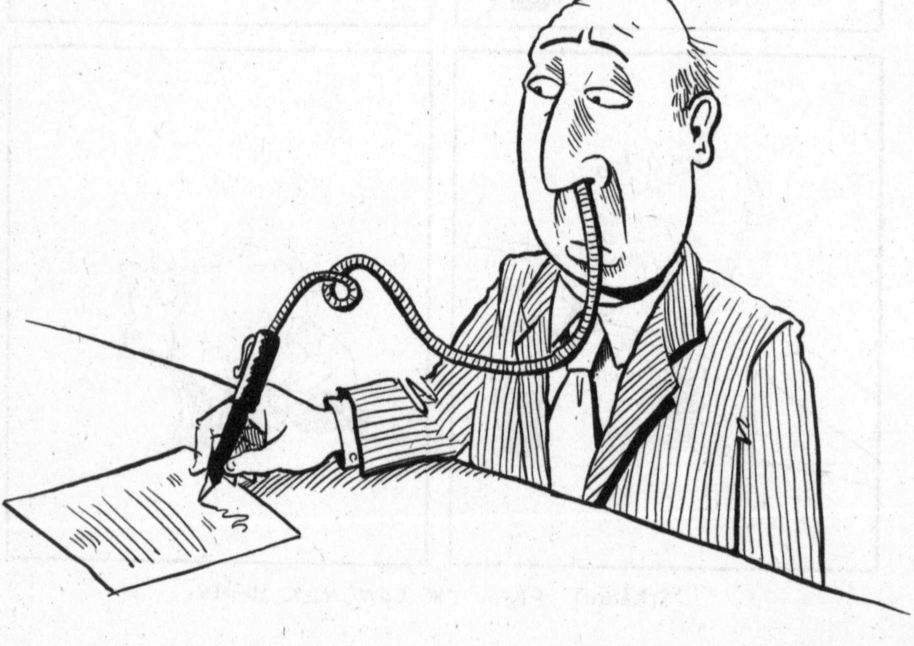

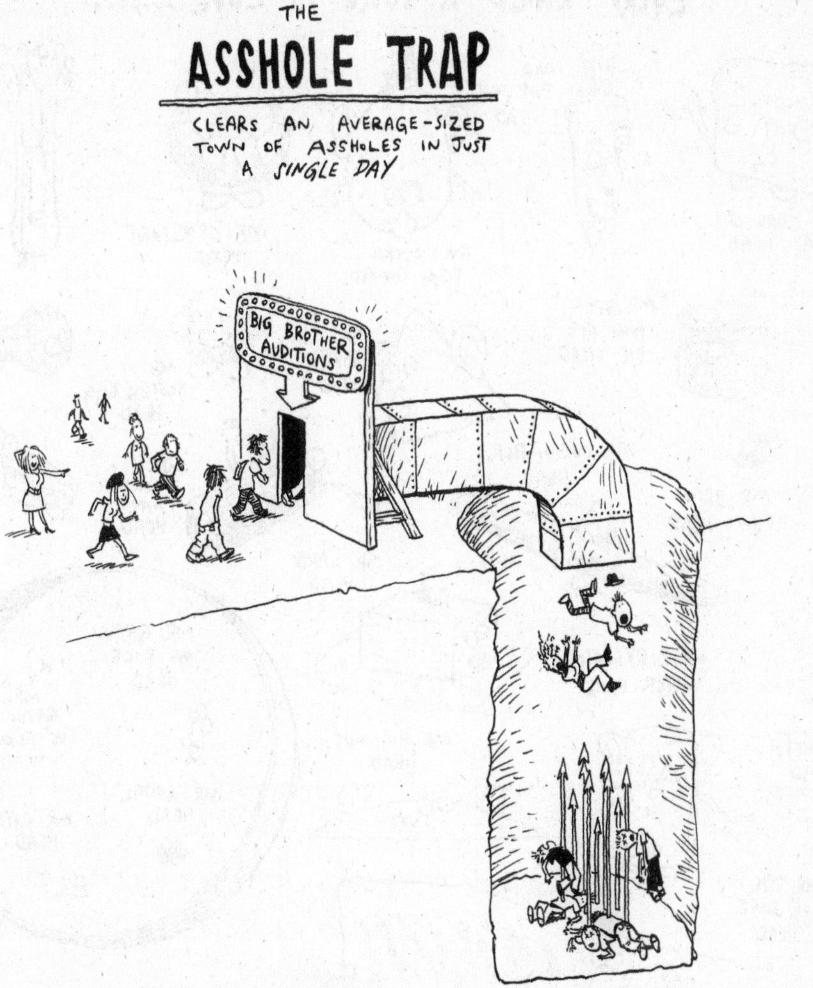
THE
ASSHOLE TRAP
CLEARS AN AVERAGE-SIZED TOWN OF ASSHOLES IN JUST A SINGLE DAY
BIG BROTHER AUDITIONS

NEW RIVALS FOR MR. POTATO HEAD

EVERY CHILD IS SURE TO LOVE........

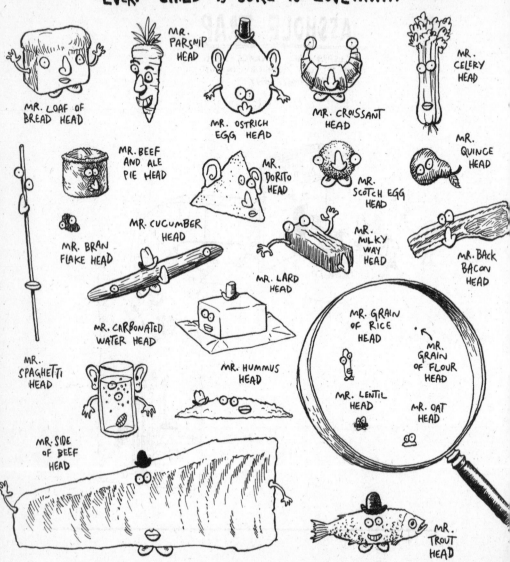

MR. LOAF OF BREAD HEAD

MR. PARSNIP HEAD

MR. OSTRICH EGG HEAD

MR. CROISSANT HEAD

MR. CELERY HEAD

MR. BEEF AND ALE PIE HEAD

MR. DORITO HEAD

MR. SCOTCH EGG HEAD

MR. QUINCE HEAD

MR. BRAN FLAKE HEAD

MR. CUCUMBER HEAD

MR. MILKY WAY HEAD

MR. BACK BACON HEAD

MR. LARD HEAD

MR. CARBONATED WATER HEAD

MR. SPAGHETTI HEAD

MR. HUMMUS HEAD

MR. GRAIN OF RICE HEAD

MR. GRAIN OF FLOUR HEAD

MR. LENTIL HEAD

MR. OAT HEAD

MR. SIDE OF BEEF HEAD

MR. TROUT HEAD

DISCOBALLS
FOR GOTH
NIGHTCLUBS

CHOPSTICK HEAVY LIFTER
FOR CHINESE BUILDING SITES

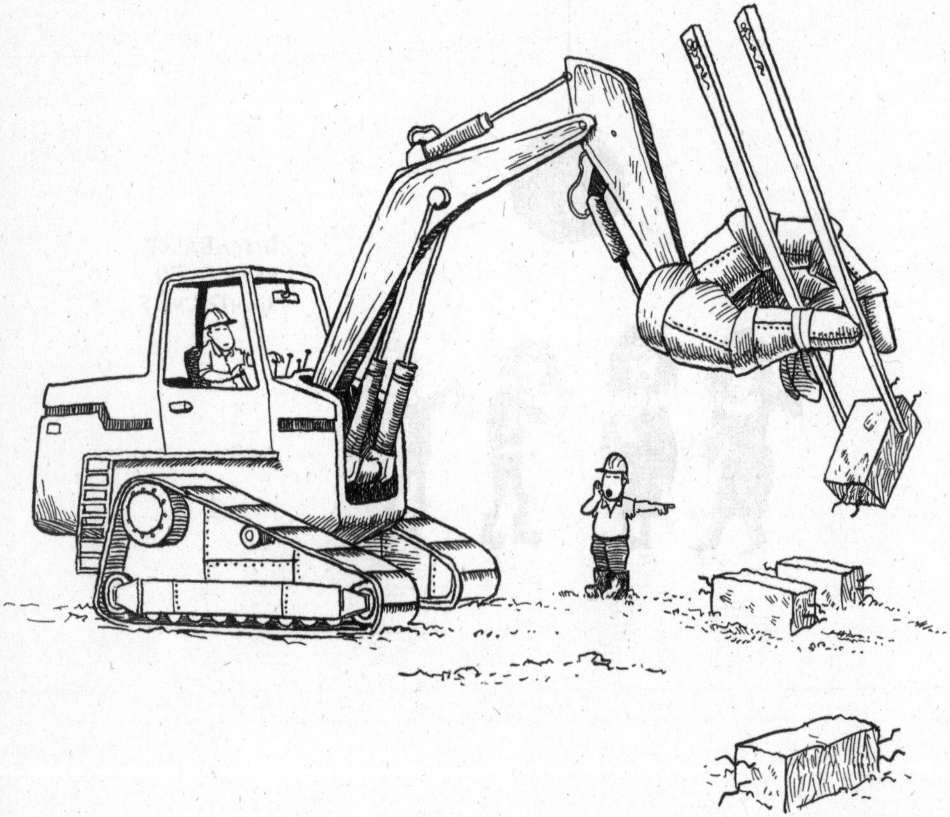

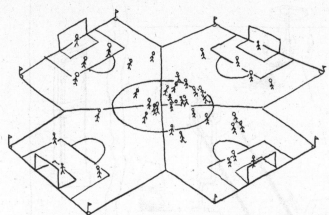

FOUR-WAY SOCCER

— DECIDES A
WORLD CUP
GROUP IN A
SINGLE
AFTERNOON

36-WAY
SOCCER

— DECIDES THE
ENTIRE
WORLD CUP
IN A SINGLE
AFTERNOON

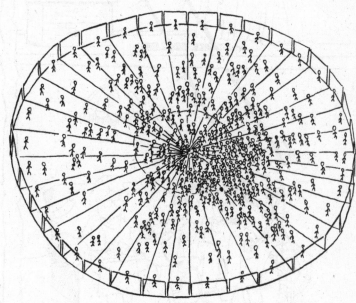

THE PIZZA LEAFLET INSTANT DISPOSAL SYSTEM

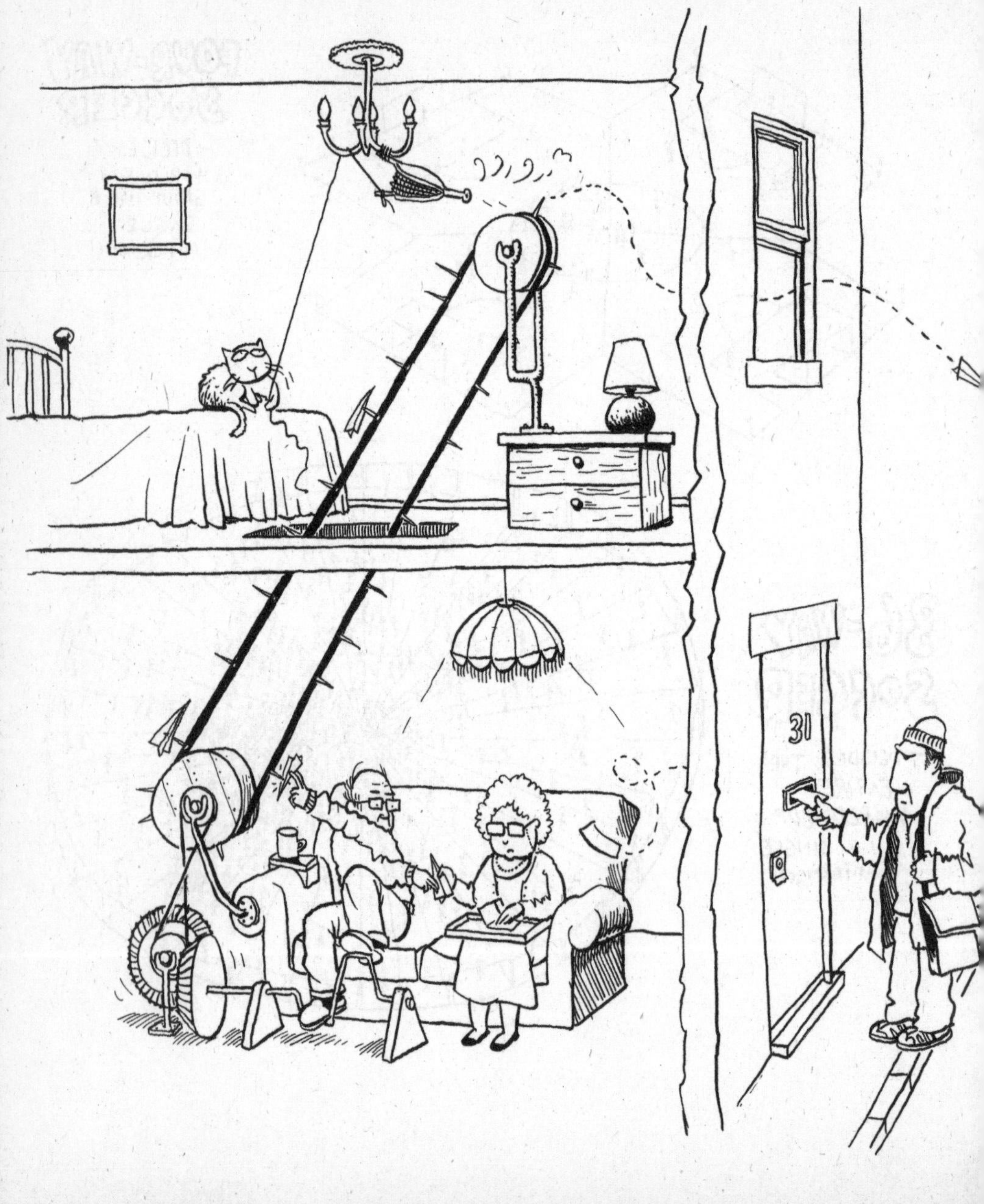
31

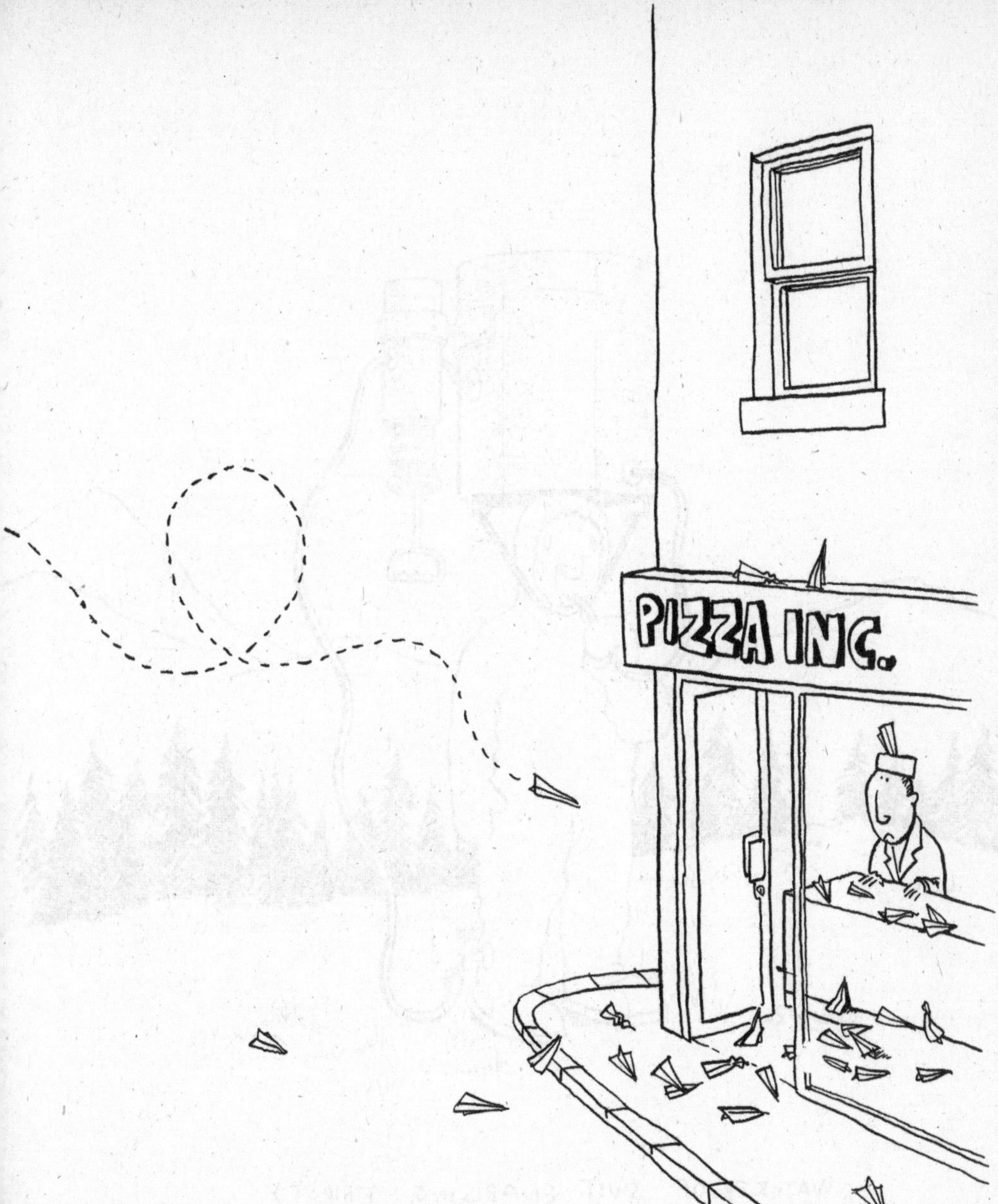
PIZZA INC.

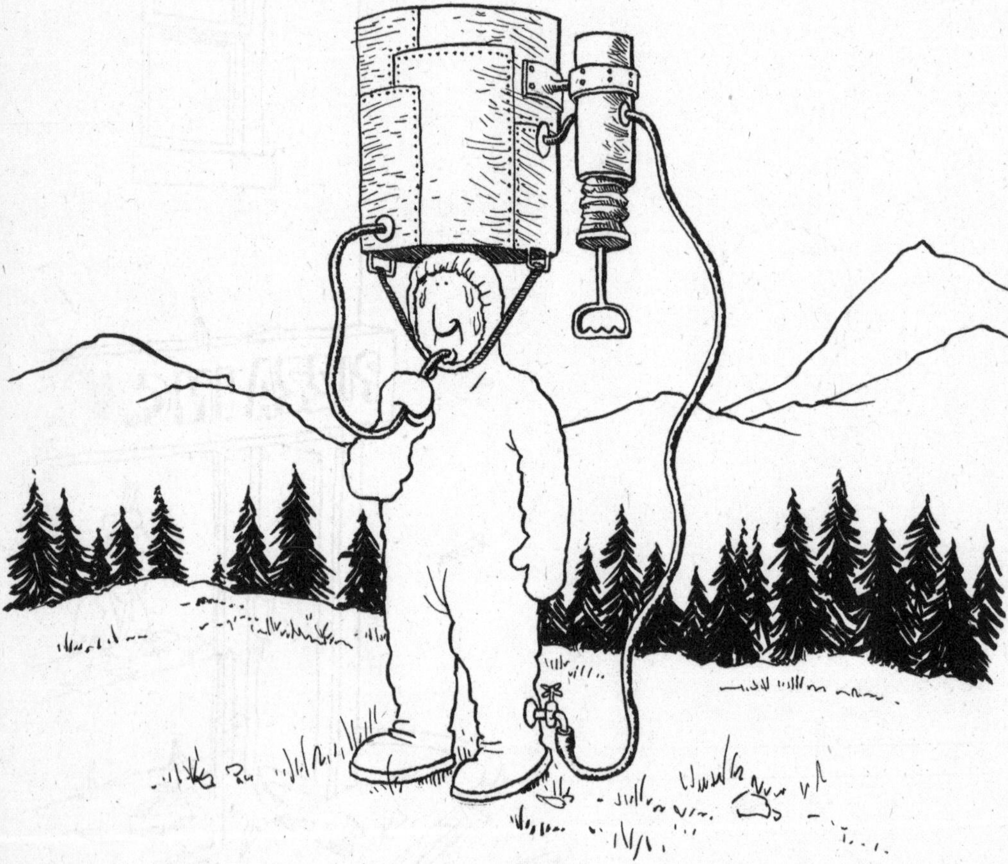

WATERPROOF SUIT ENABLING THIRSTY HIKERS TO DRINK THEIR OWN SWEAT

SYSTEM #1 FOR SWIFT JUSTICE FOR MOPED THIEVES

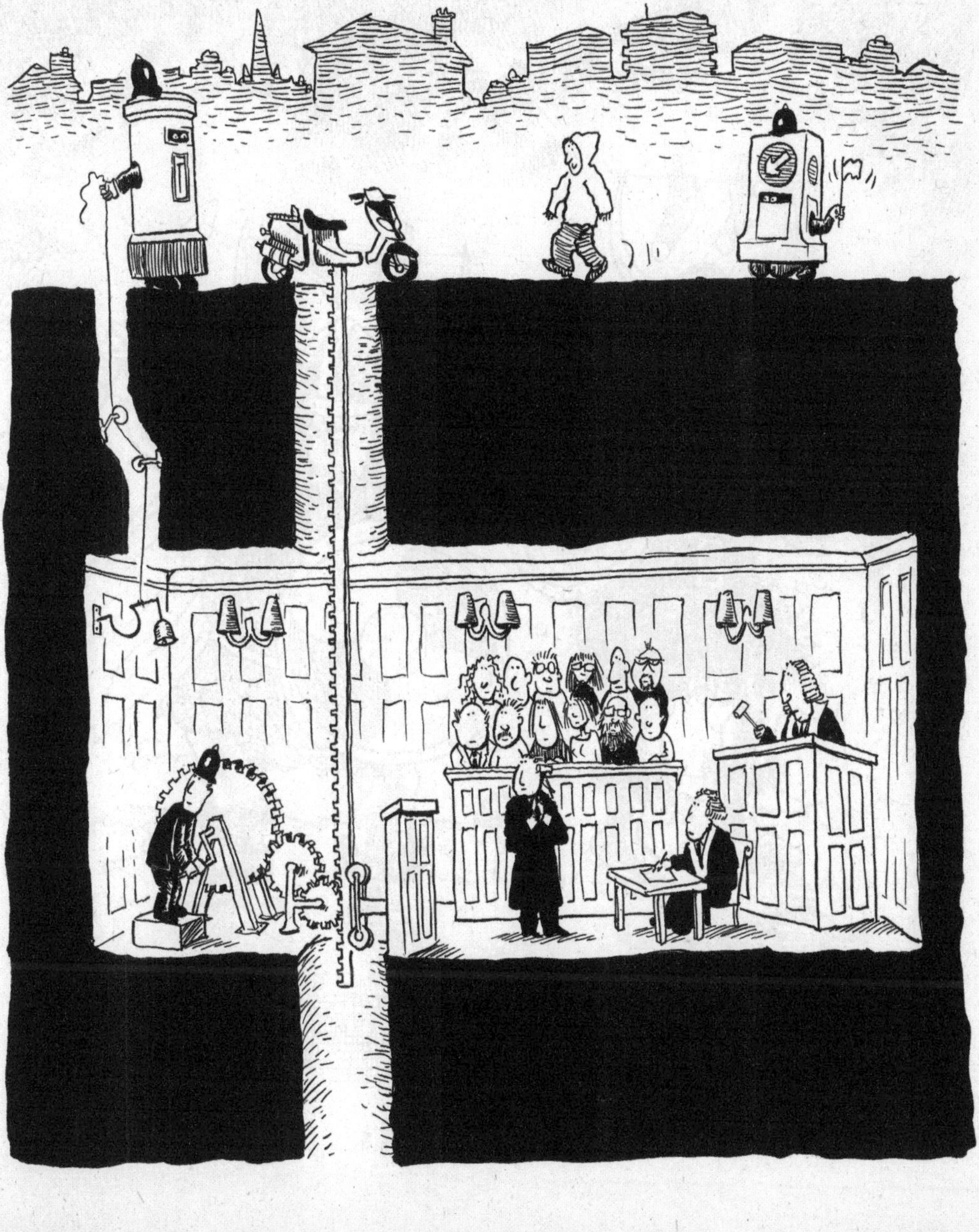

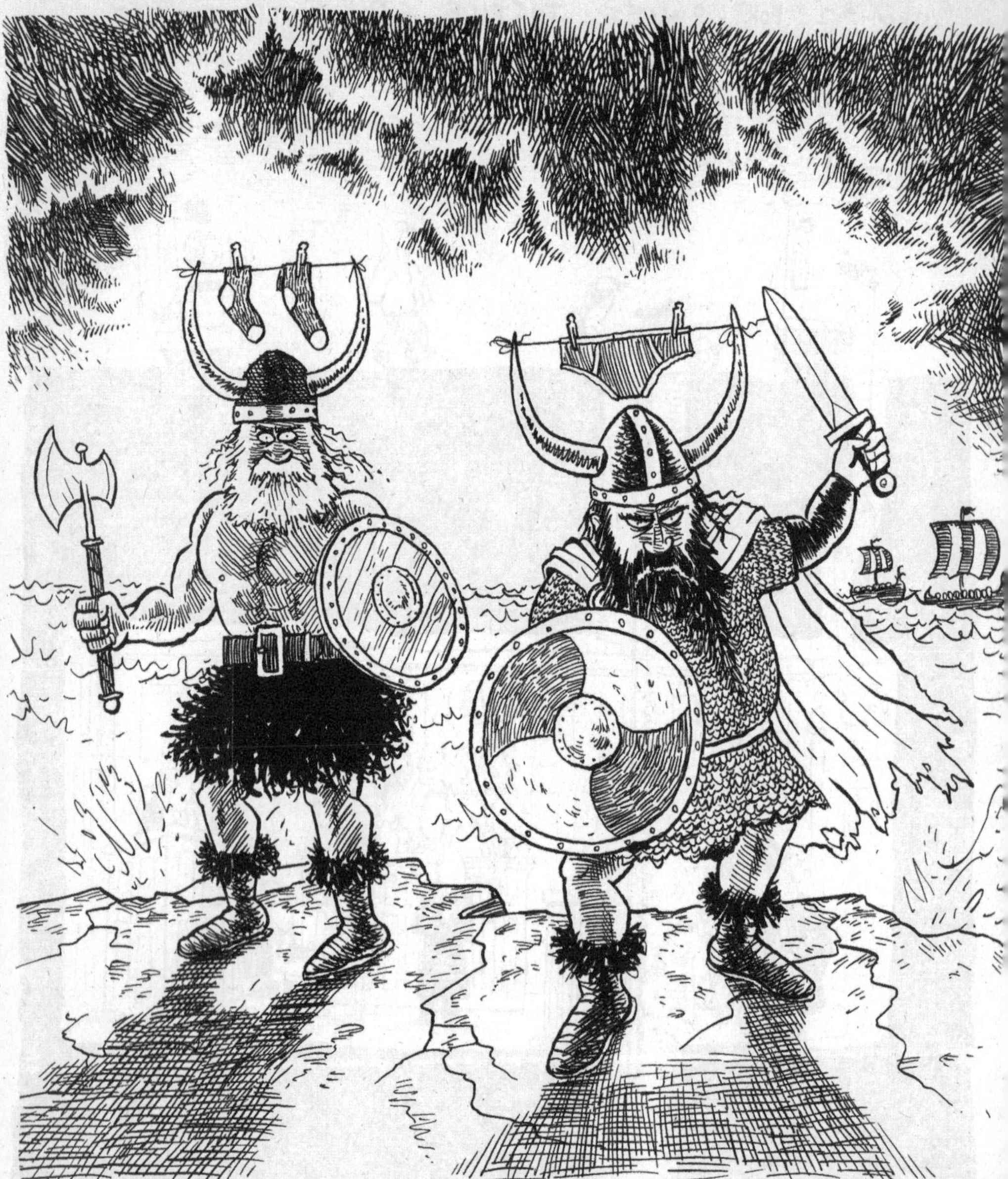

WASHING LINES FOR VIKINGS

SYSTEM FOR BEATING TRAFFIC JAMS

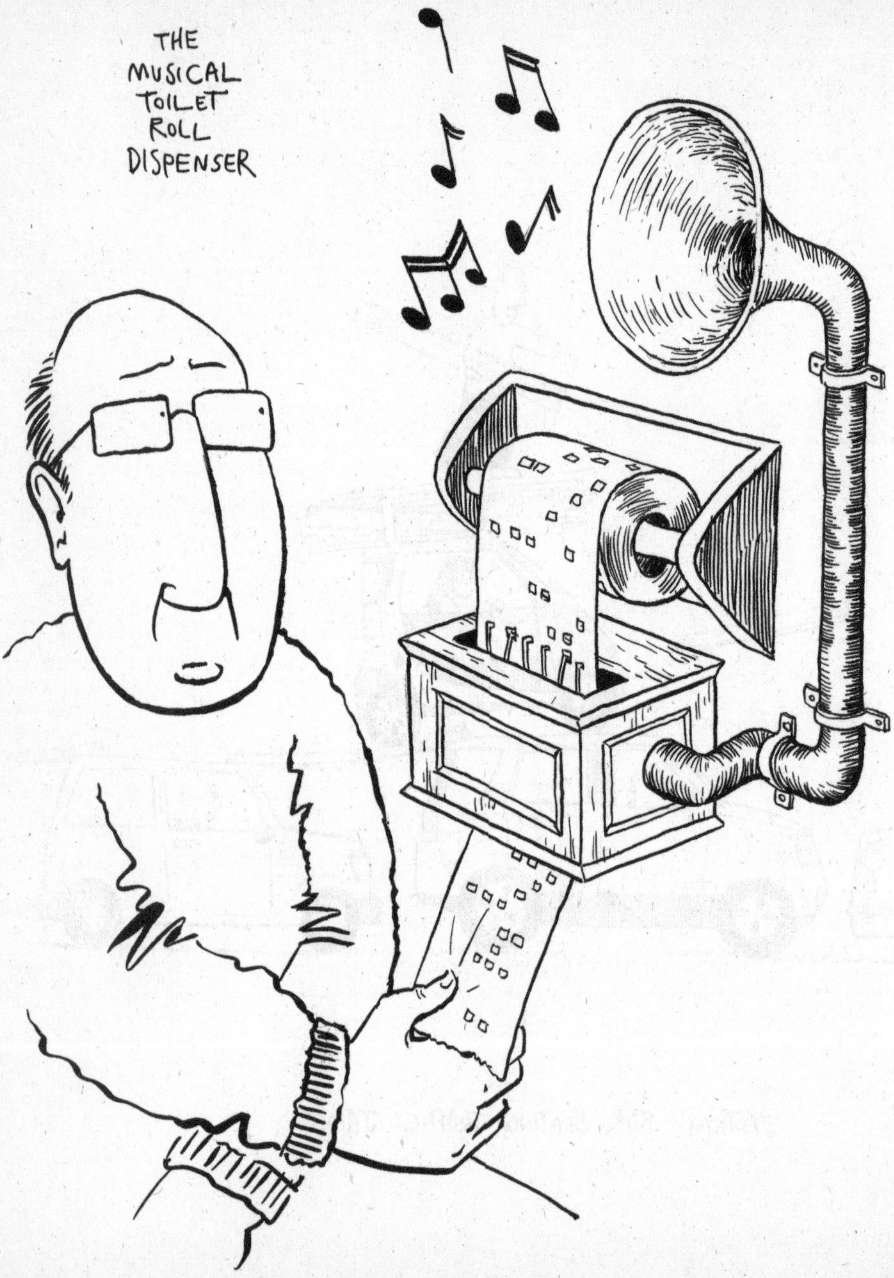
THE MUSICAL TOILET ROLL DISPENSER

THE "ASCEND 'N' READ" NOVEL FOR VERY LONG ESCALATORS

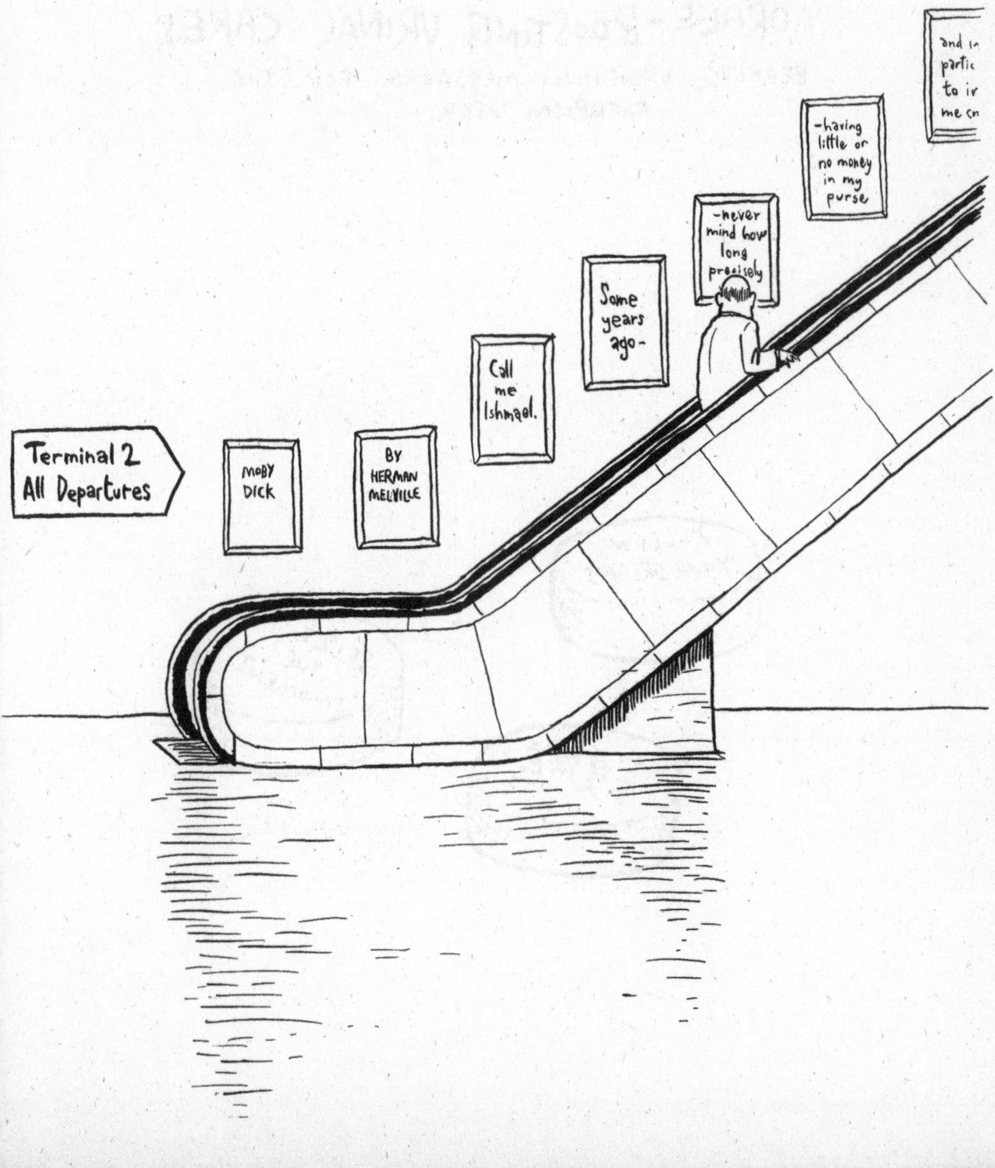

Terminal 2
All Departures
MOBY DICK
BY HERMAN MELVILLE
Call me Ishmael.
Some years ago-
-never mind how long precisely
-having little or no money in my purse

MORALE-BOOSTING URINAL CAKES

BEARING UPLIFTING MESSAGES FOR THE BATHROOM USER

FOLLOW YOUR DREAMS
SEIZE THE MOMENT
JUST BE YOUR SELF

APPARATUS FOR CROSSING MOTORWAYS SAFELY ON FOOT

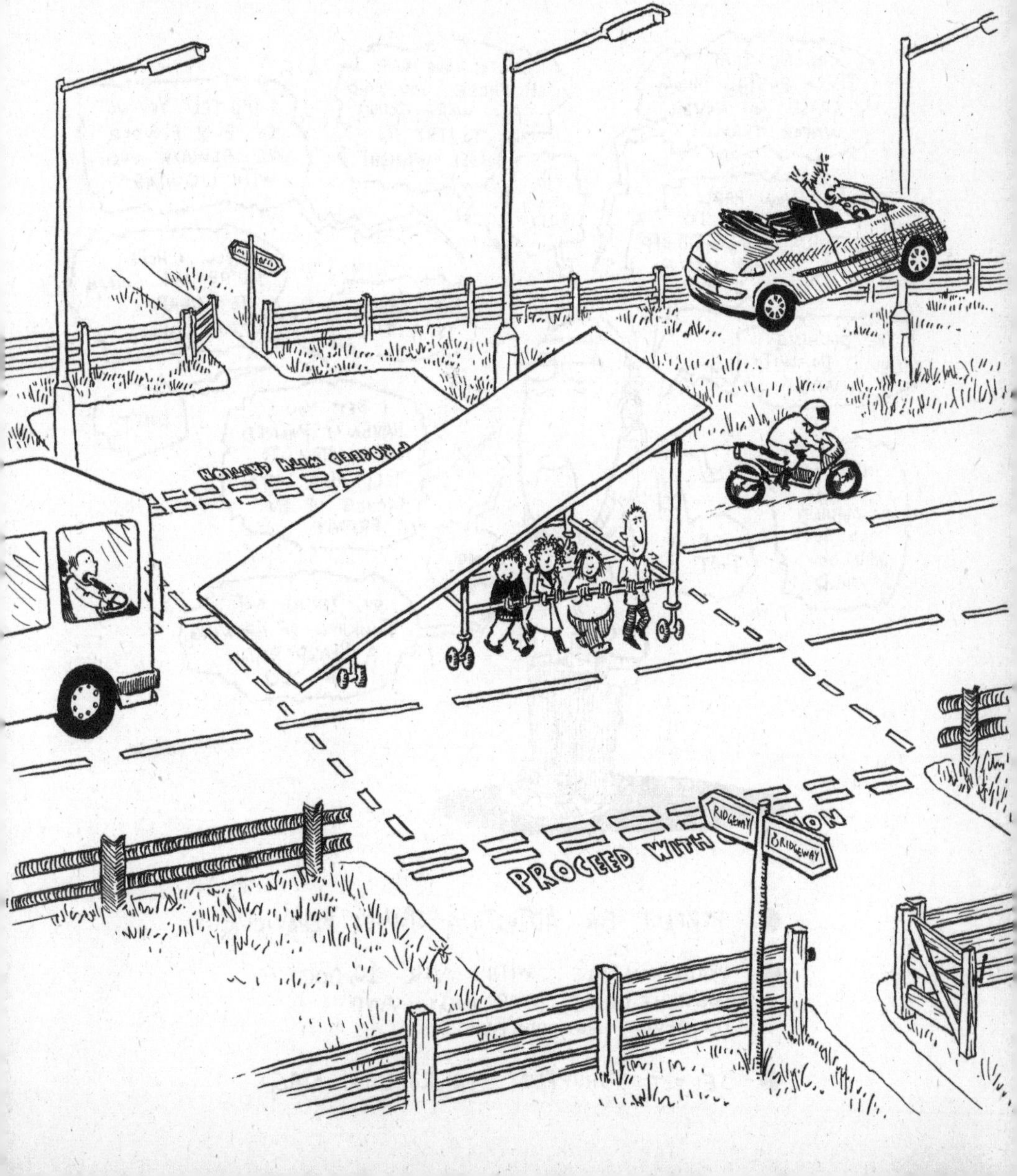

PROCEED WITH CAUTION
RIDGEWAY
RIDGEWAY
PROCEED WITH

THE Nagpod™

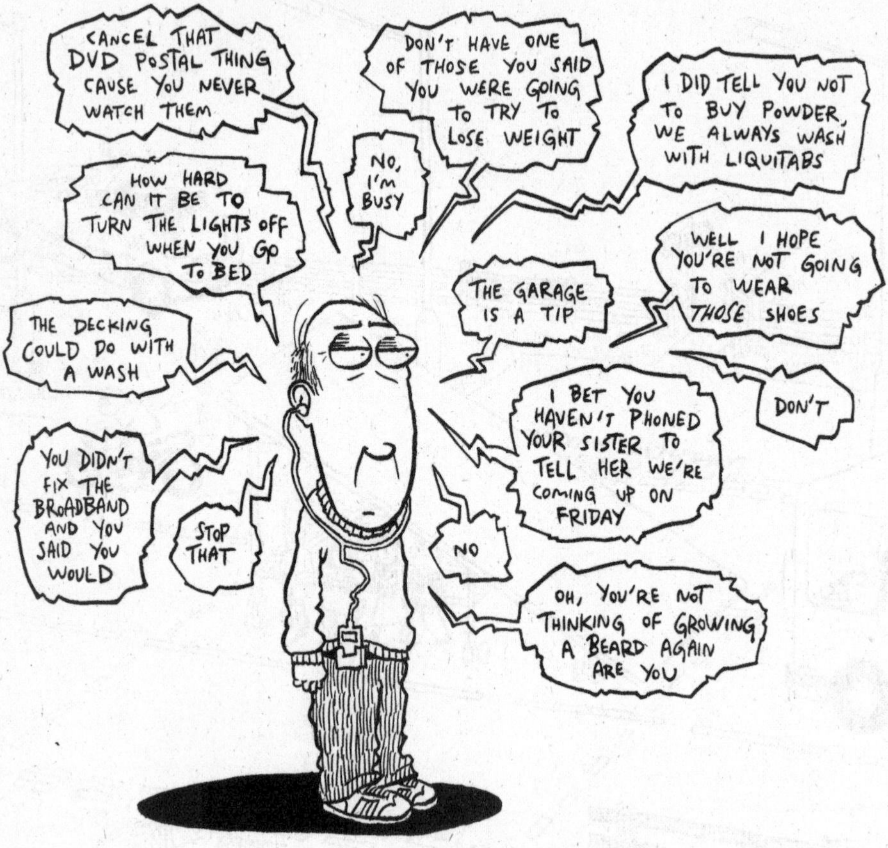

CANCEL THAT DVD POSTAL THING CAUSE YOU NEVER WATCH THEM
DON'T HAVE ONE OF THOSE YOU SAID YOU WERE GOING TO TRY TO LOSE WEIGHT
I DID TELL YOU NOT TO BUY POWDER, WE ALWAYS WASH WITH LIQUITABS
NO, I'M BUSY
HOW HARD CAN IT BE TO TURN THE LIGHTS OFF WHEN YOU GO TO BED
WELL I HOPE YOU'RE NOT GOING TO WEAR *THOSE* SHOES
THE GARAGE IS A TIP
THE DECKING COULD DO WITH A WASH
DON'T
I BET YOU HAVEN'T PHONED YOUR SISTER TO TELL HER WE'RE COMING UP ON FRIDAY
YOU DIDN'T FIX THE BROADBAND AND YOU SAID YOU WOULD
STOP THAT
NO
OH, YOU'RE NOT THINKING OF GROWING A BEARD AGAIN ARE YOU

- PERFECT FOR ADJUSTING SPOUSE'S BEHAVIOUR
- PROGRAMMABLE WITH OVER 10,000 INSTRUCTIONS, WARNINGS AND HELPFUL ADMONITIONS
- SELECT "SHUFFLE" FOR RANDOM NAGS

AUTO—SCOOPER FOR DOGS

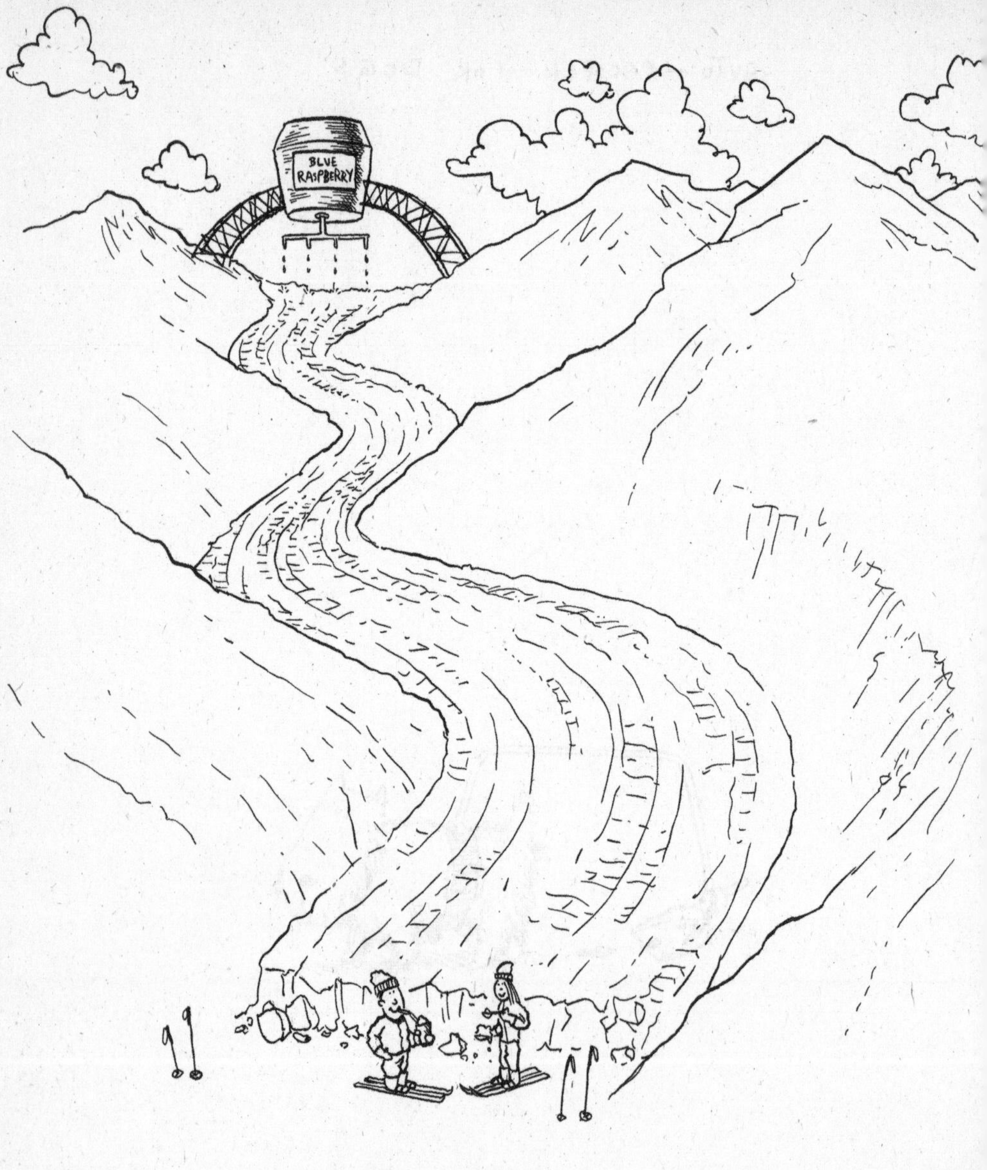
BLUE RASPBERRY

FLAVOURED GLACIERS

SYSTEM #2 FOR SWIFT JUSTICE FOR MOPED THIEVES

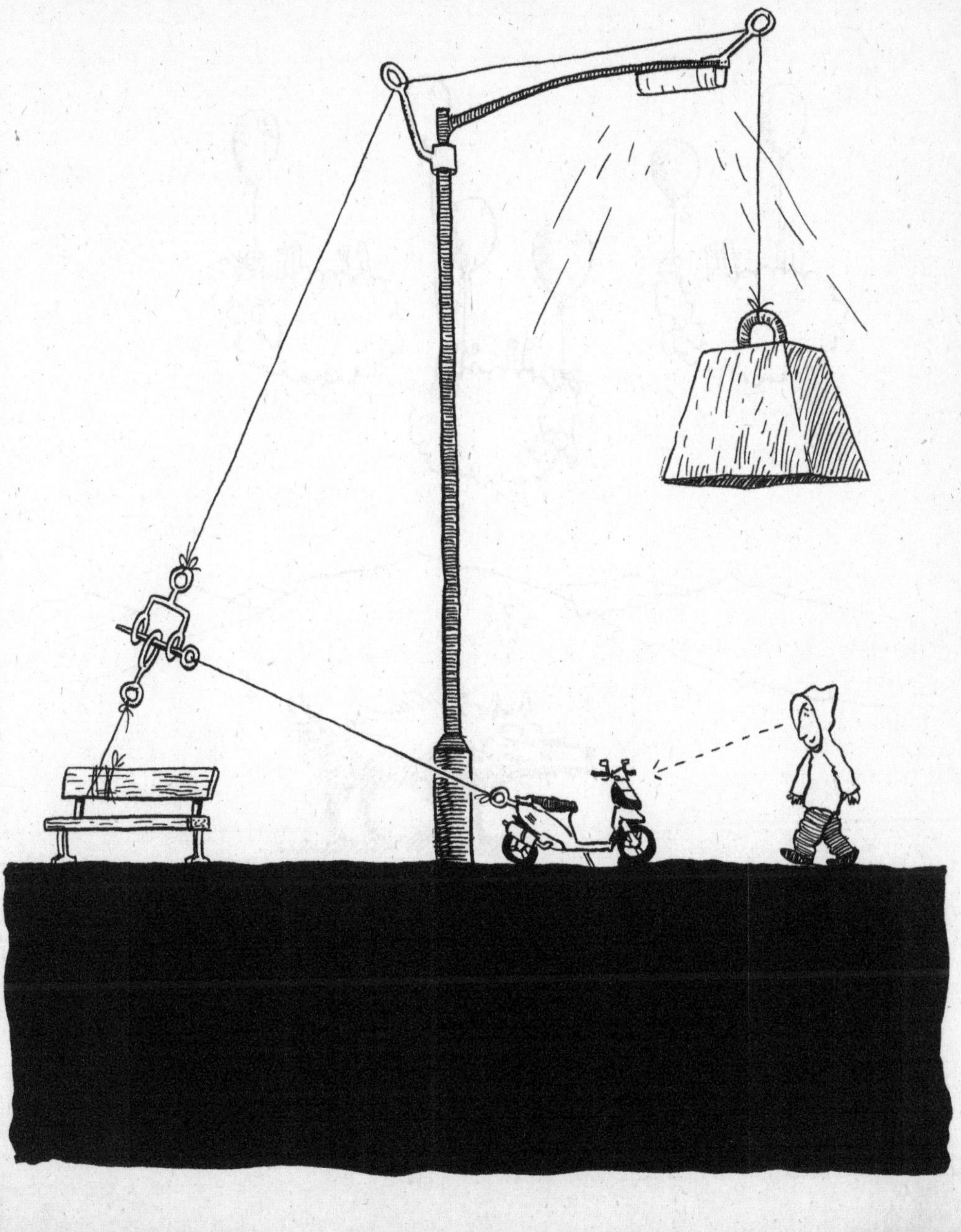

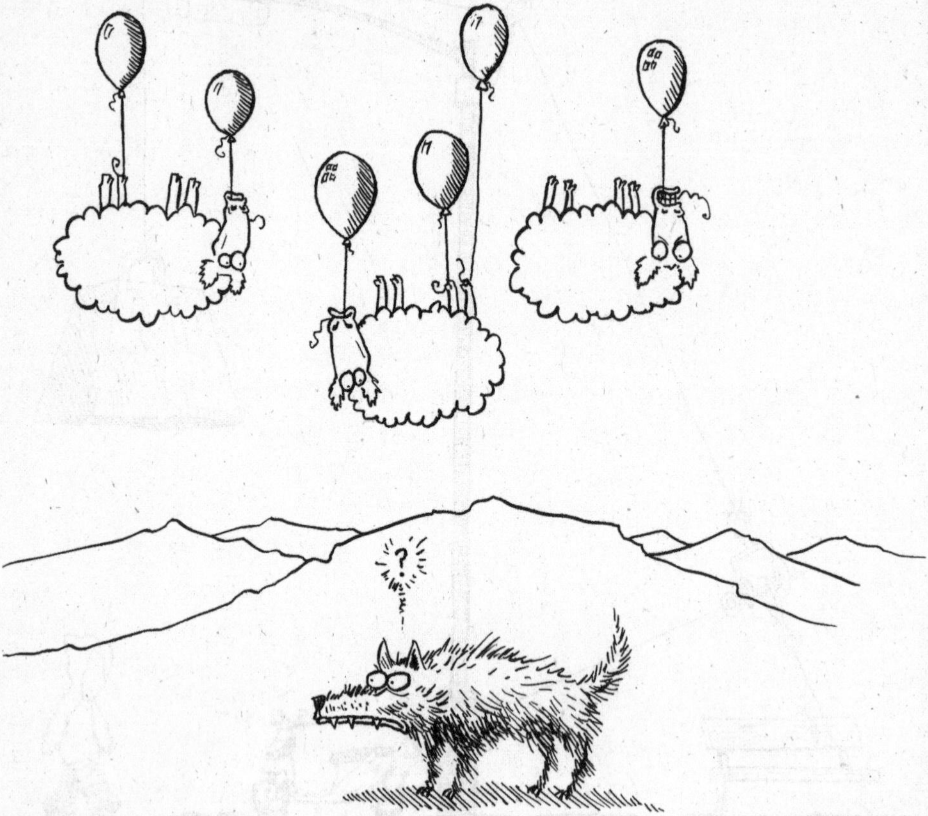
?

METHOD FOR SHEEP TO DISGUISE THEMSELVES AS SMALL FLUFFY CLOUDS WHEN THREATENED BY A WOLF

THE

TOASTER-LAPTOP

FOR CONVENIENT SURFING 'N' SNACKING

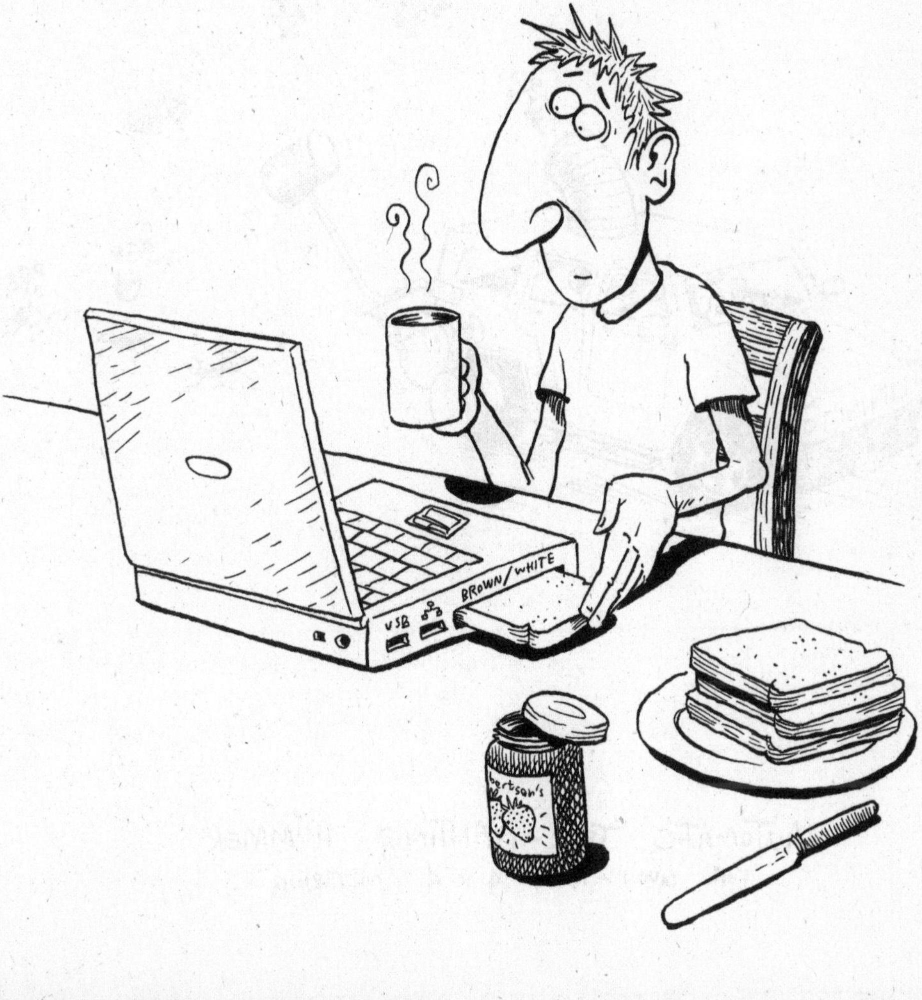
BROWN/WHITE
USB
bertson's

AUTOMATIC TREE-PLANTING HUMMER
FOR GUILT-FREE 4 x 4 MOTORING

SURVEILLANCE BAUBLES

-TELL SANTA IF YOU'VE BEEN BAD OR GOOD
INSTANTLY

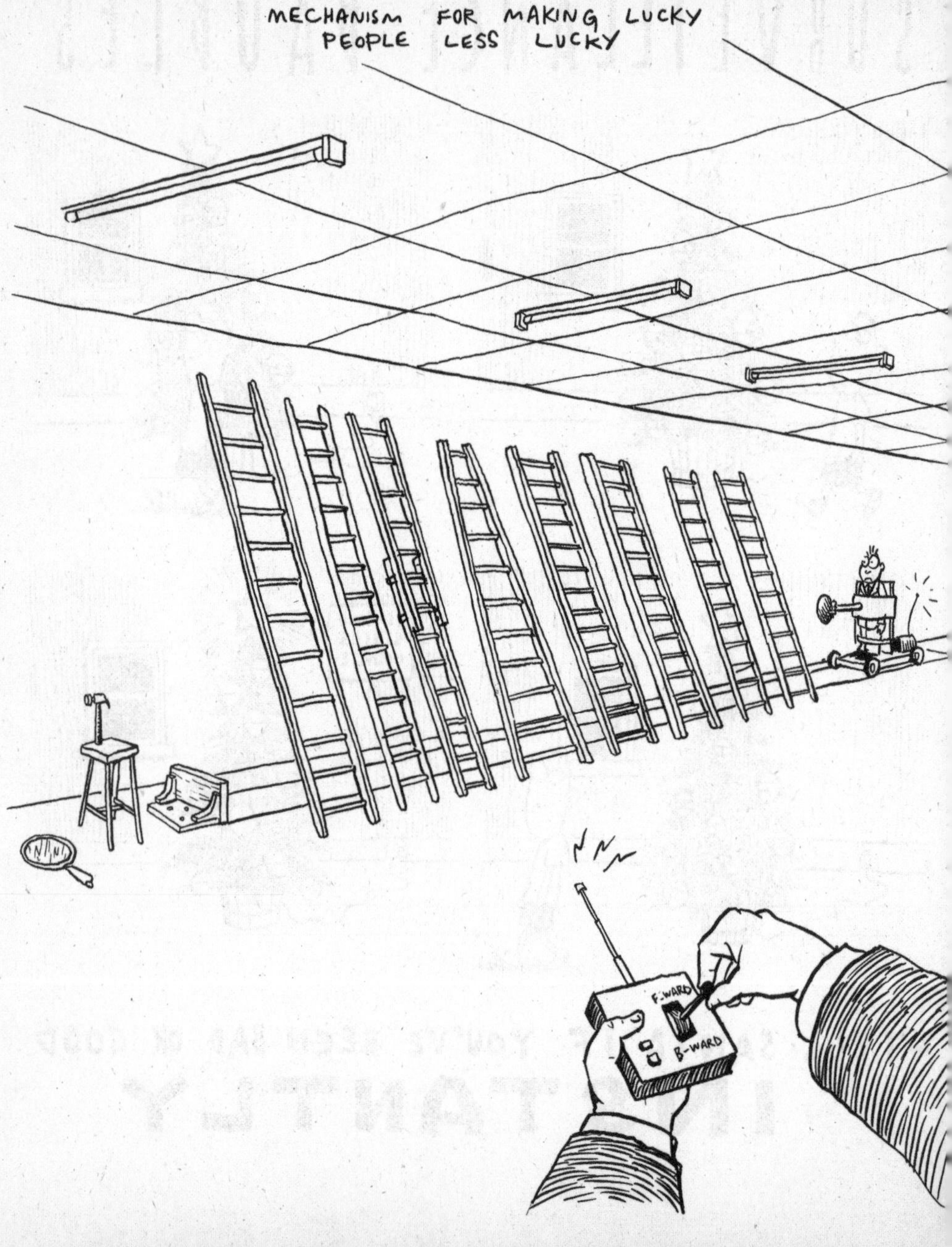
MECHANISM FOR MAKING LUCKY PEOPLE LESS LUCKY
F-WARD
B-WARD

MOEBIUS STRIP MAPS FOR HIKERS WHO ENJOY AN INTELLECTUAL CHALLENGE

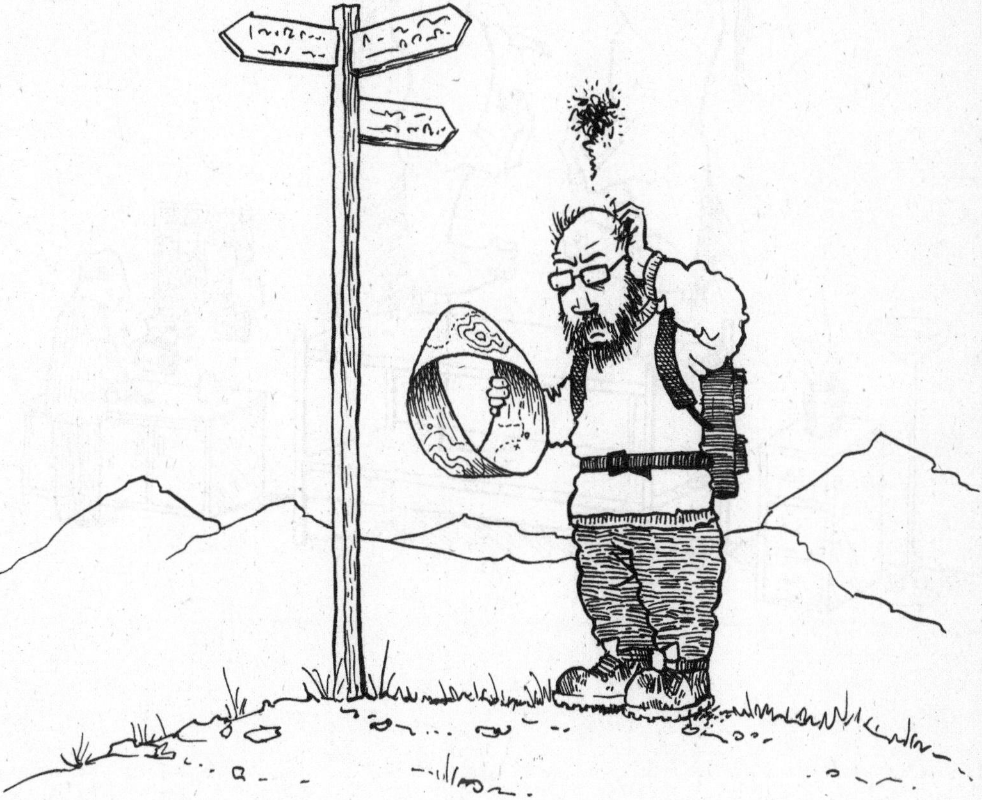

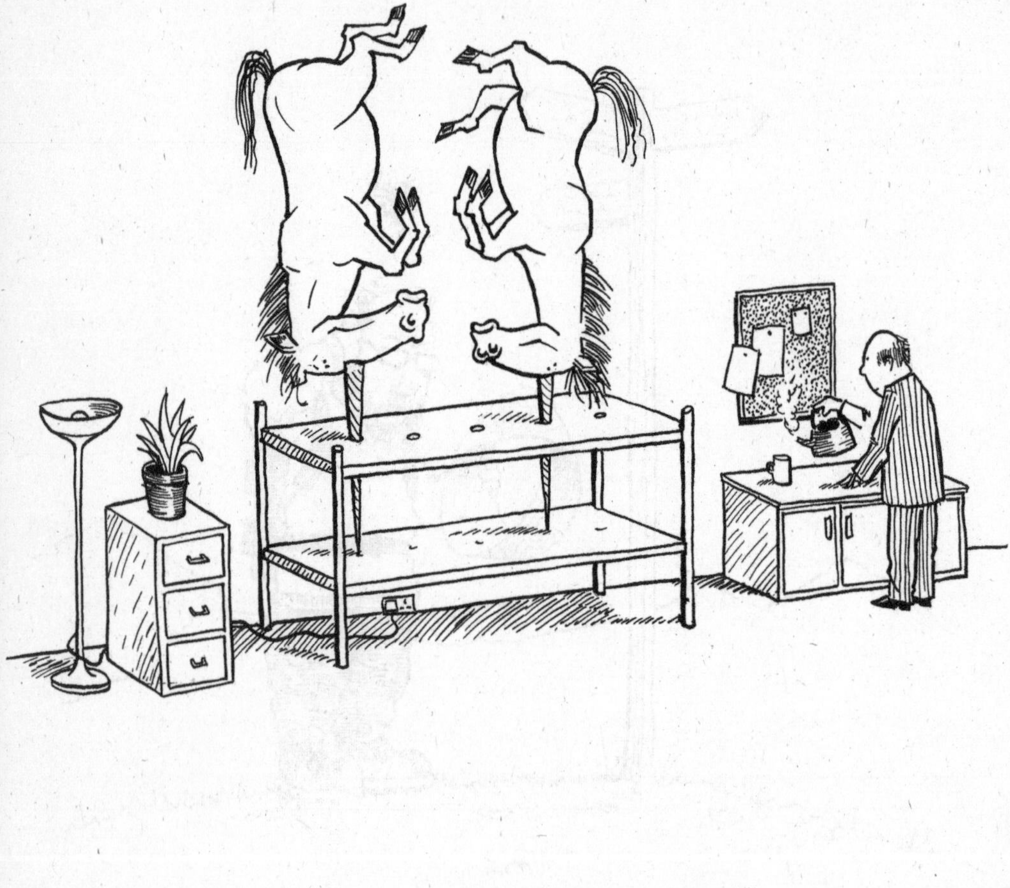

UNICORN STORAGE RACK

'COP CATAPULT' FOR RAPID RESPONSE TO URBAN CRIME

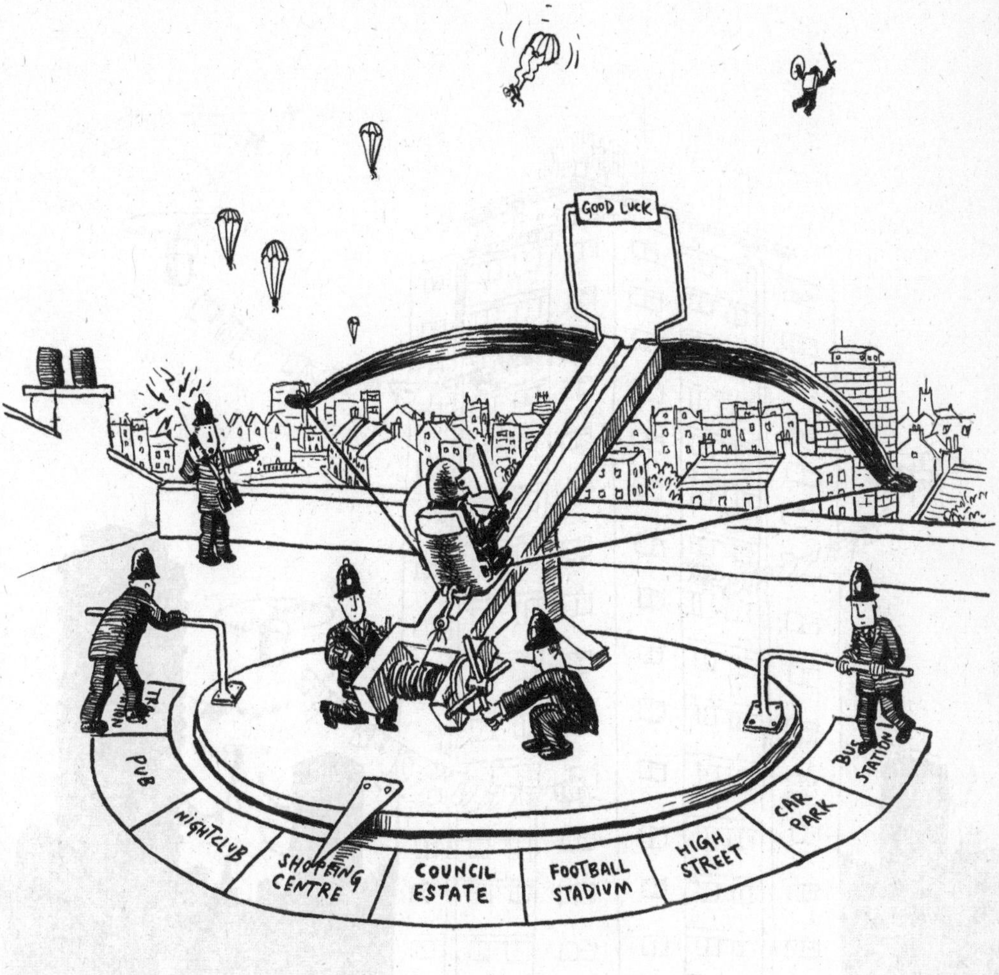
GOOD LUCK
PUB
NIGHTCLUB
CENTRE
COUNCIL ESTATE
FOOTBALL STADIUM
HIGH STREET
CAR PARK
BUS STATION

THE HELI-WASHING LINE FOR PEOPLE IN TALL BUILDINGS

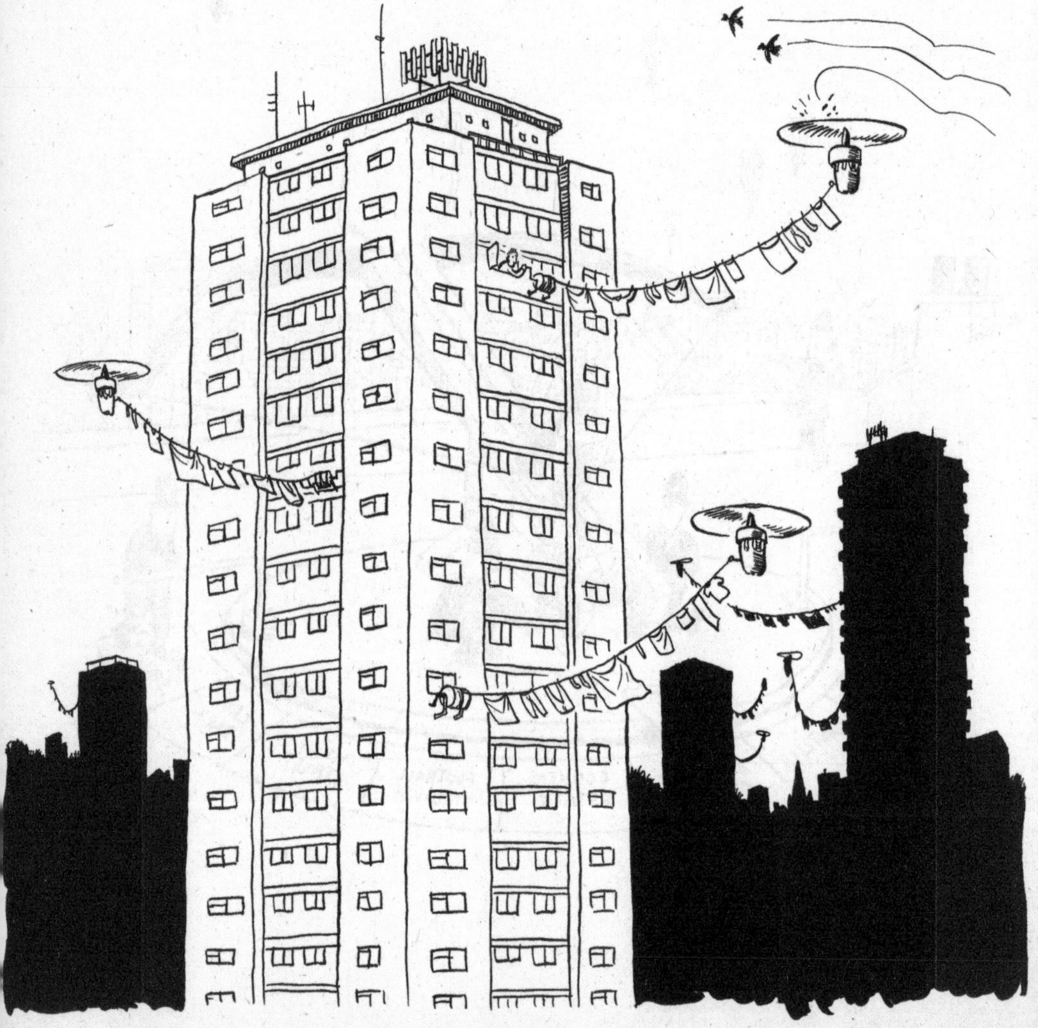

D.I.Y. DENTISTRY

CHECK UP

DRILLING

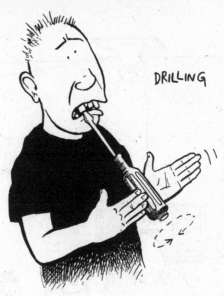

EXTRACTION METHOD #1

REPLACEMENT

EXTRACTION METHOD #2

CAMEL IDENTIFYING MACHINE FOR THE BUSY ZOOKEEPER

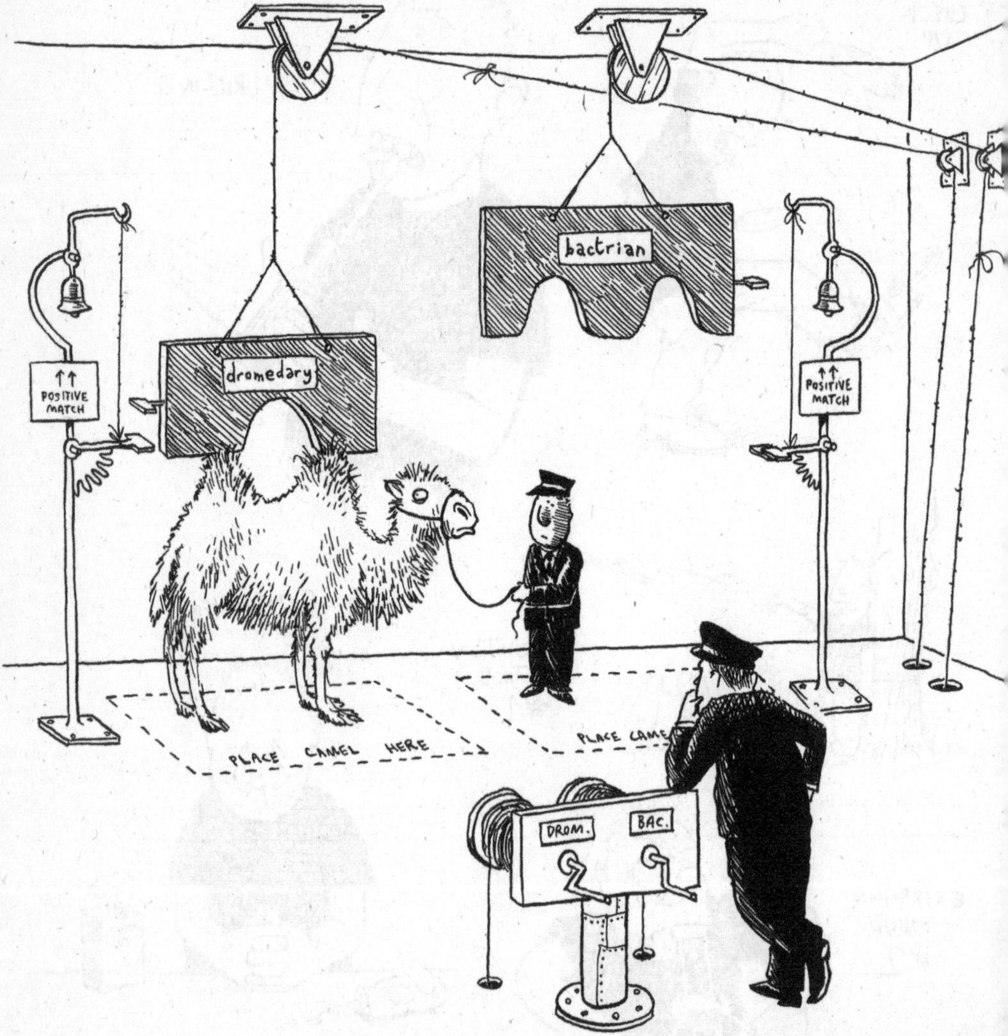
dromedary
bactrian
↑↑ POSITIVE MATCH
↑↑ POSITIVE MATCH
PLACE CAMEL HERE
PLACE CAME
DROM.
BAC.

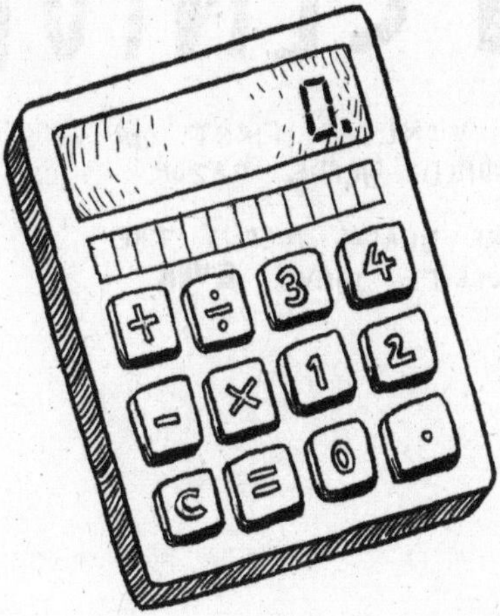
0.
4
3
÷
+
2
1
×
-
.
0
=
C

A CALCULATOR FOR
PEOPLE WHO DON'T
LIKE NUMBERS
BIGGER THAN FOUR

THE MACH CENTURY™

- THE WORLD'S FIRST ONE HUNDRED BLADE RAZOR
- MORE BLADES MEANS THE CLOSEST SHAVE **EVER**

BEFORE

AFTER

THE ROBOTIC BURGER BUGGY

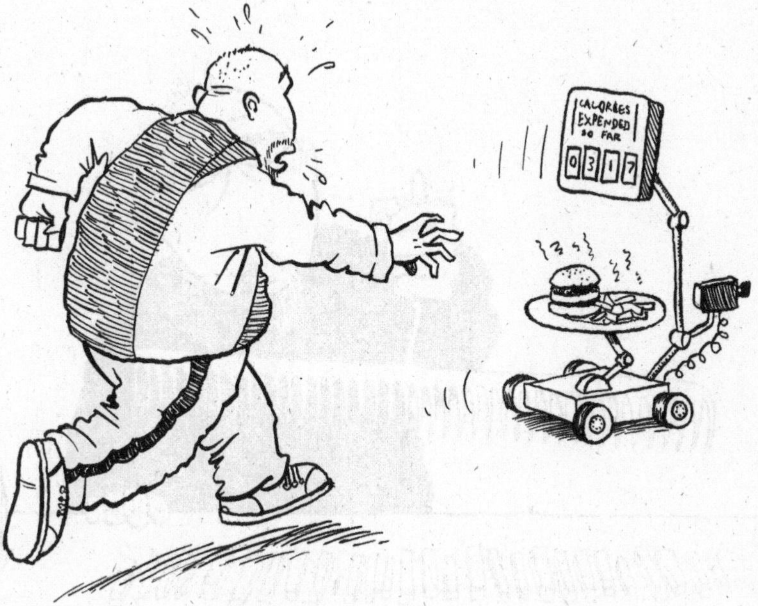
CALORIES EXPENDED SO FAR
0317

WON'T LET ITSELF BE CAUGHT UNTIL YOU'VE JOGGED OFF ALL THE CALORIES YOU'RE ABOUT TO EAT

A FORK DESIGNED TO PICK UP AN
ENTIRE PORTION OF FRIES IN ONE GO

(NOTE: FRIES MAY
REQUIRE ALIGNMENT)

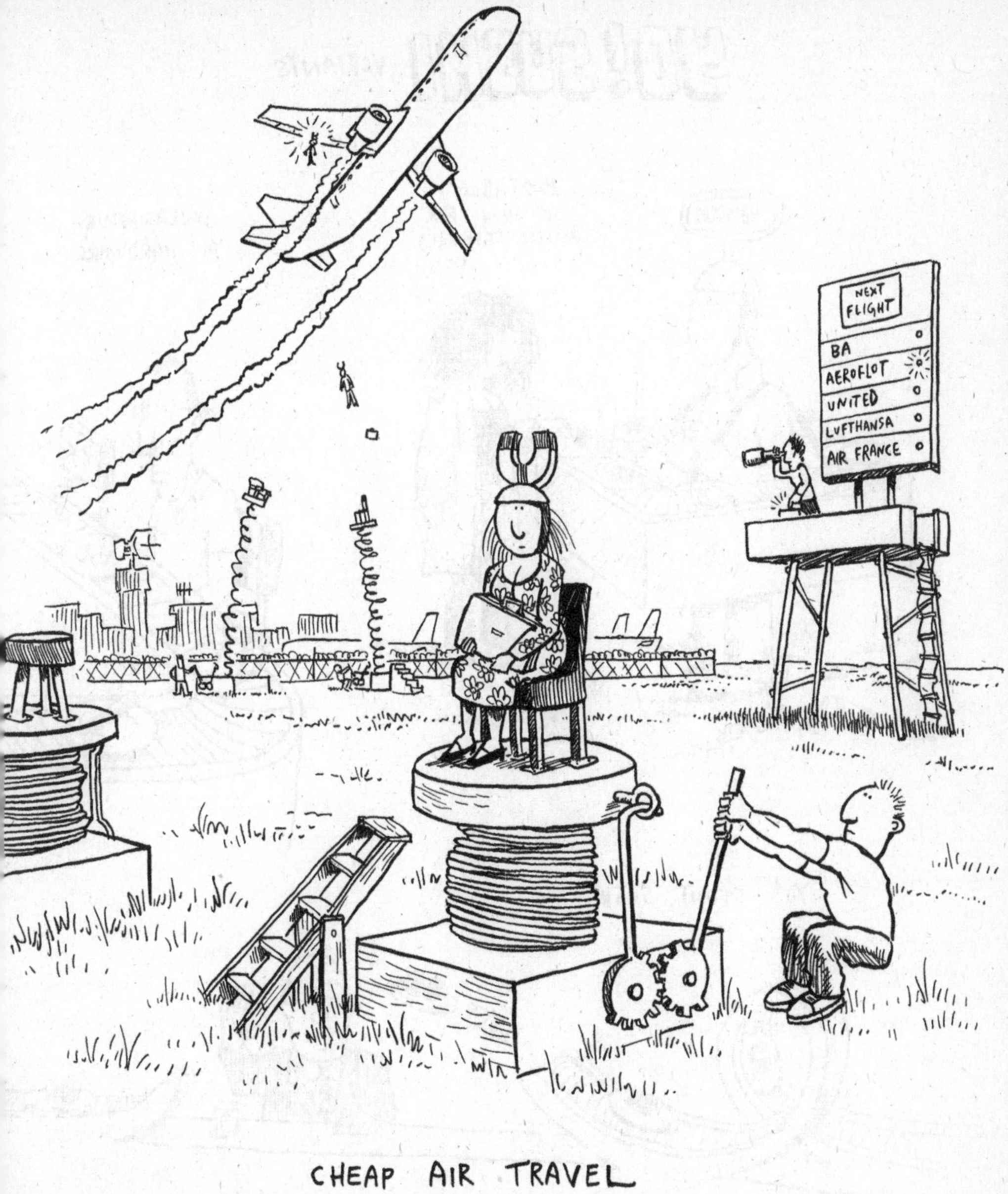
NEXT FLIGHT
BA
AEROFLOT
UNITED
LUFTHANSA
AIR FRANCE

CHEAP AIR TRAVEL

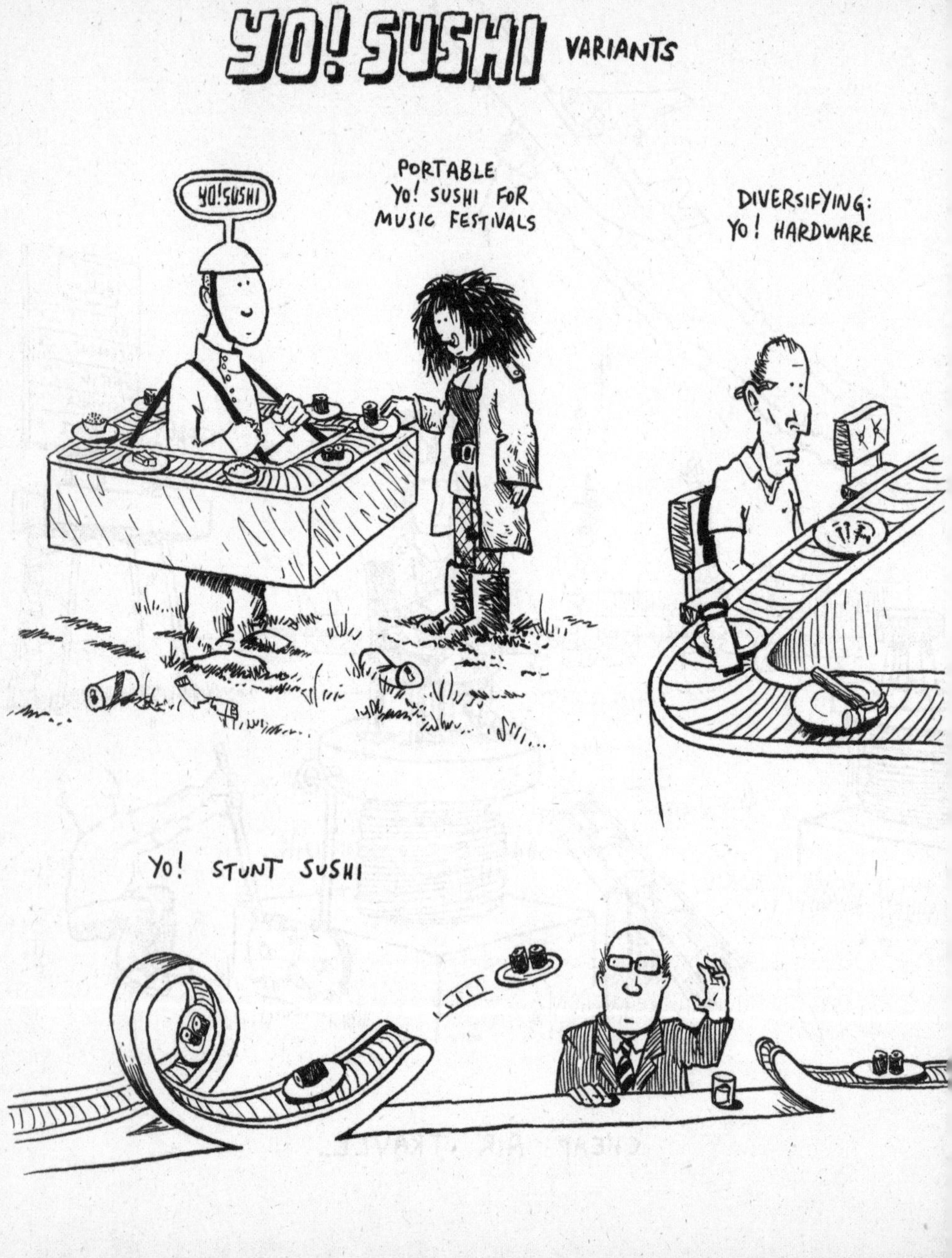
YO! SUSHI VARIANTS
PORTABLE YO! SUSHI FOR MUSIC FESTIVALS
YO!SUSHI
DIVERSIFYING: YO! HARDWARE
YO! STUNT SUSHI

A WEB INTERFACE ESPECIALLY FOR PIGS

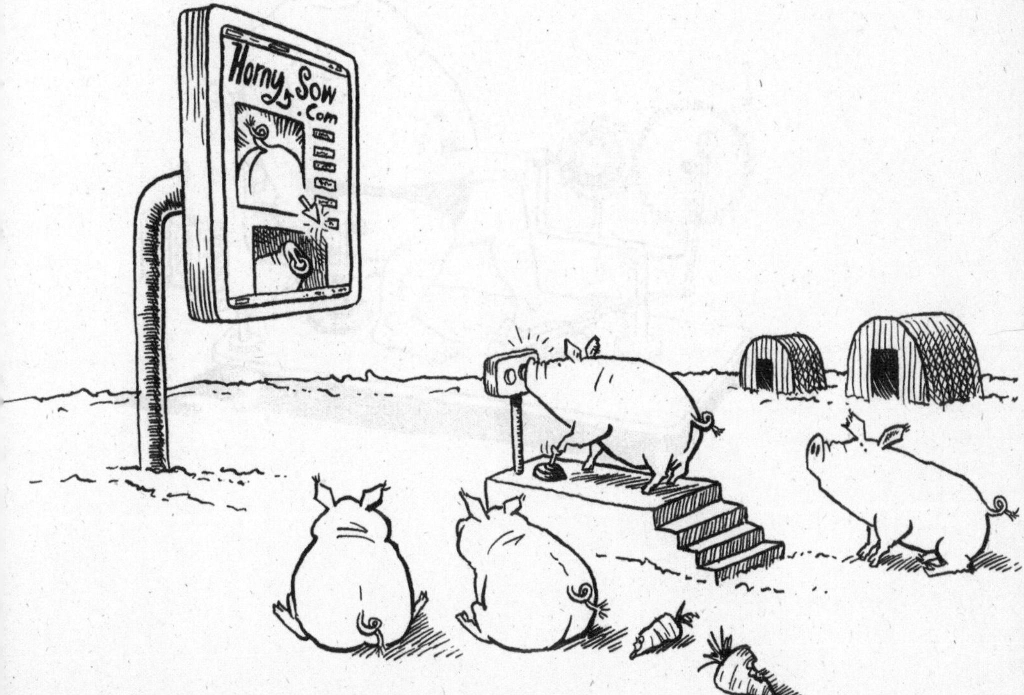

HornySow.com

TREADLE-POWERED BELLY BUTTON DE-FLUFFER

LIGHT BRISTLE
MEDIUM BRISTLE
STIFF BRISTLE

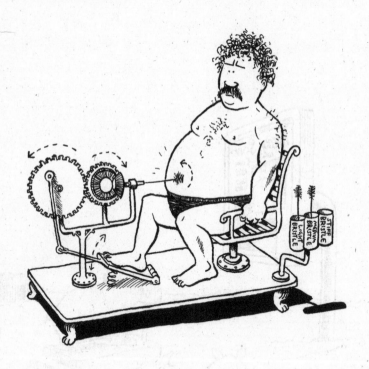

PIGEON-PROOF STATUES

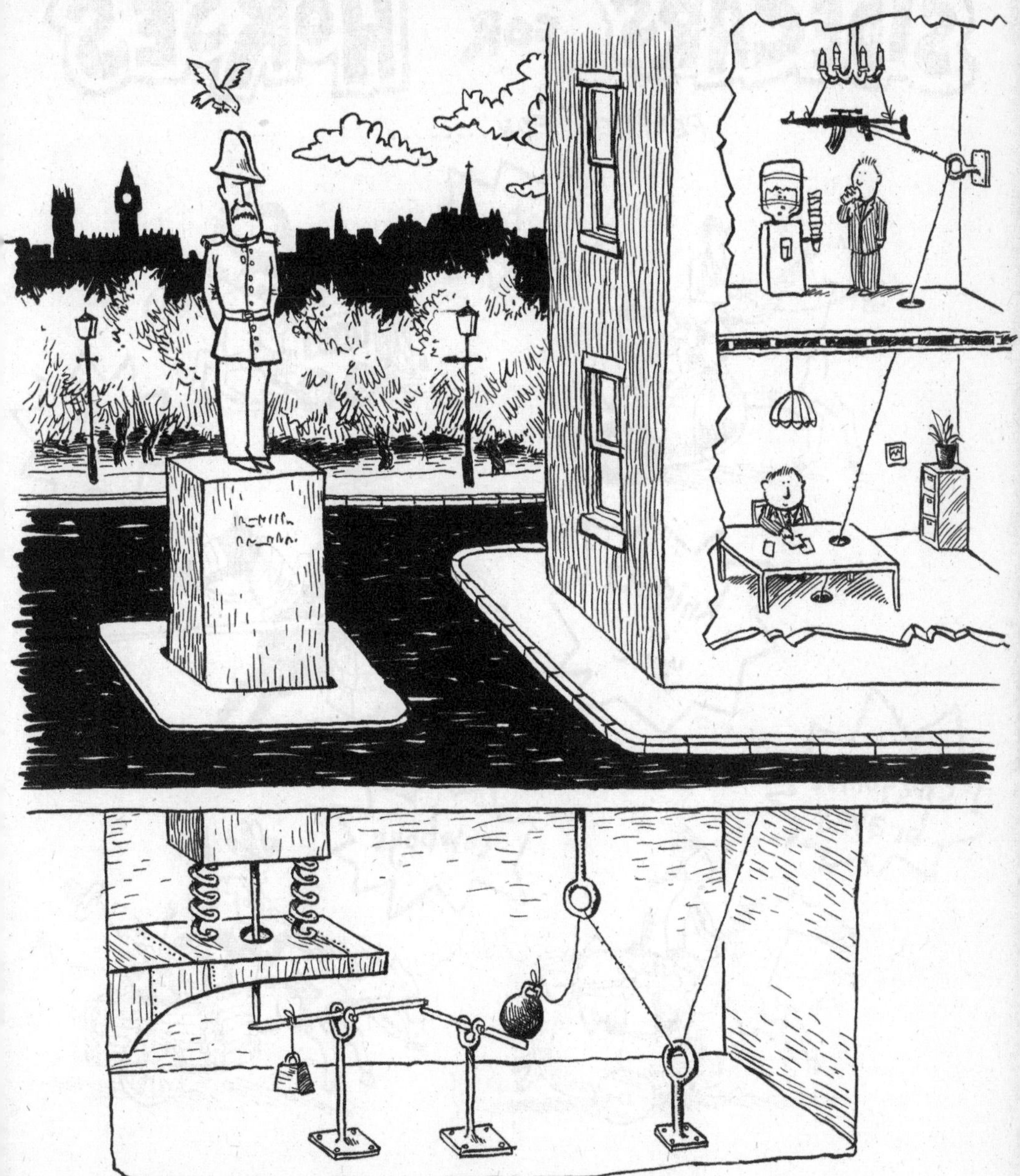

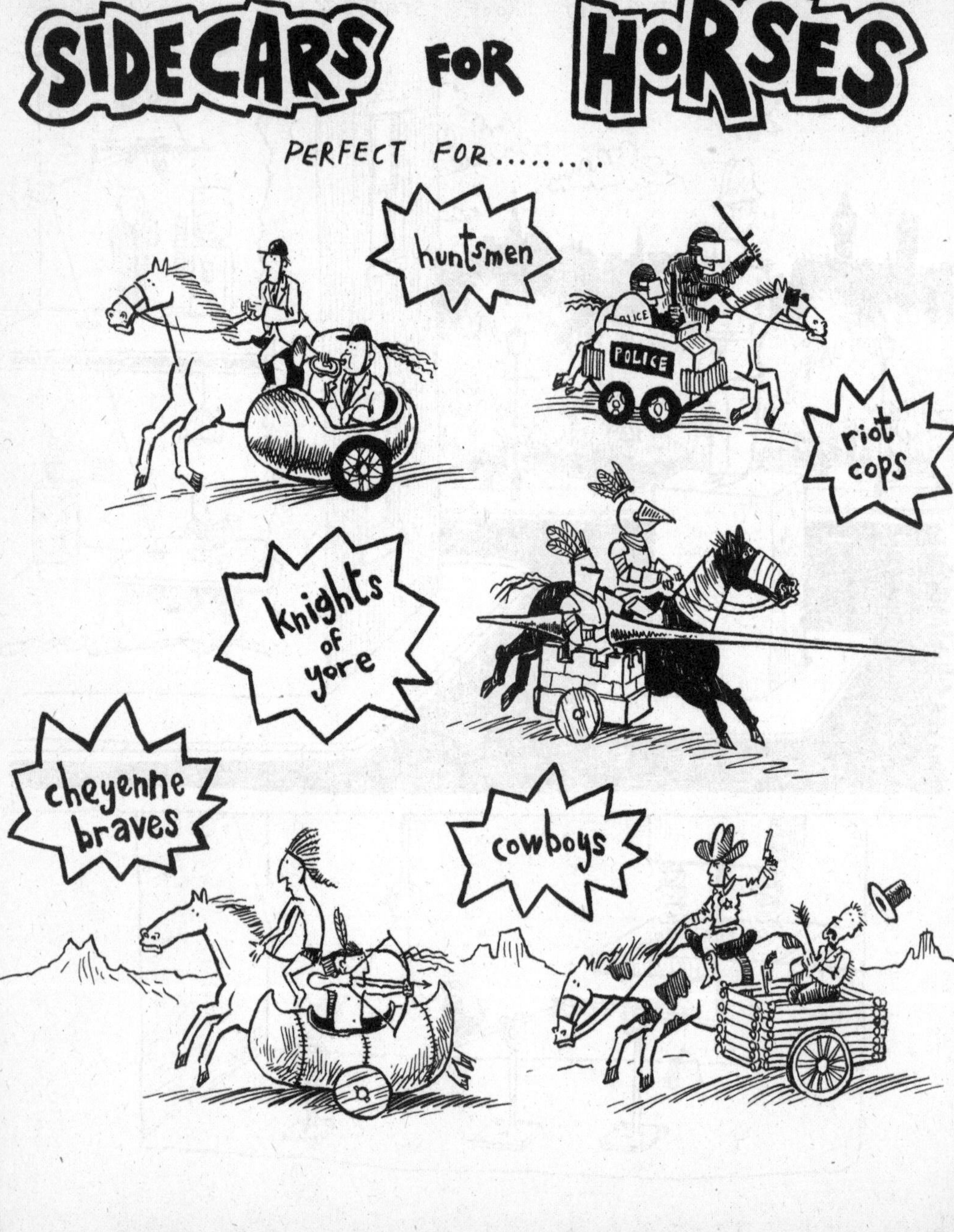
SIDECARS FOR HORSES
PERFECT FOR.........
huntsmen
POLICE
POLICE
riot cops
knights of yore
cheyenne braves
cowboys

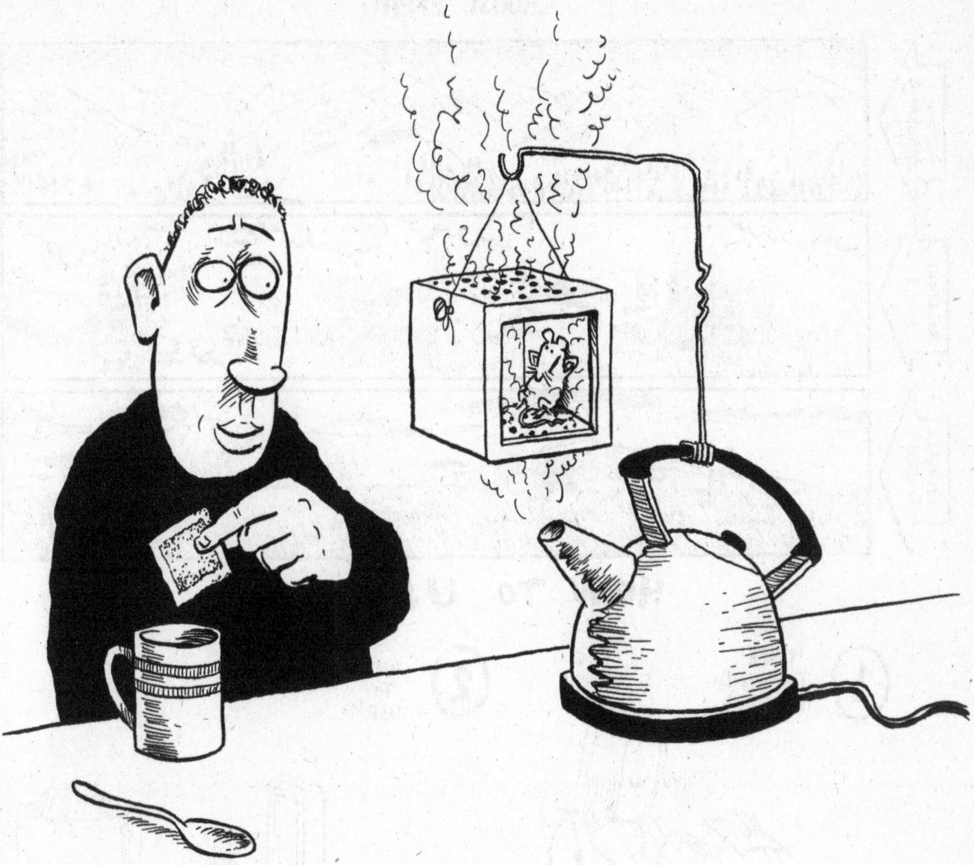

STEAM BATH FOR A PET MOUSE

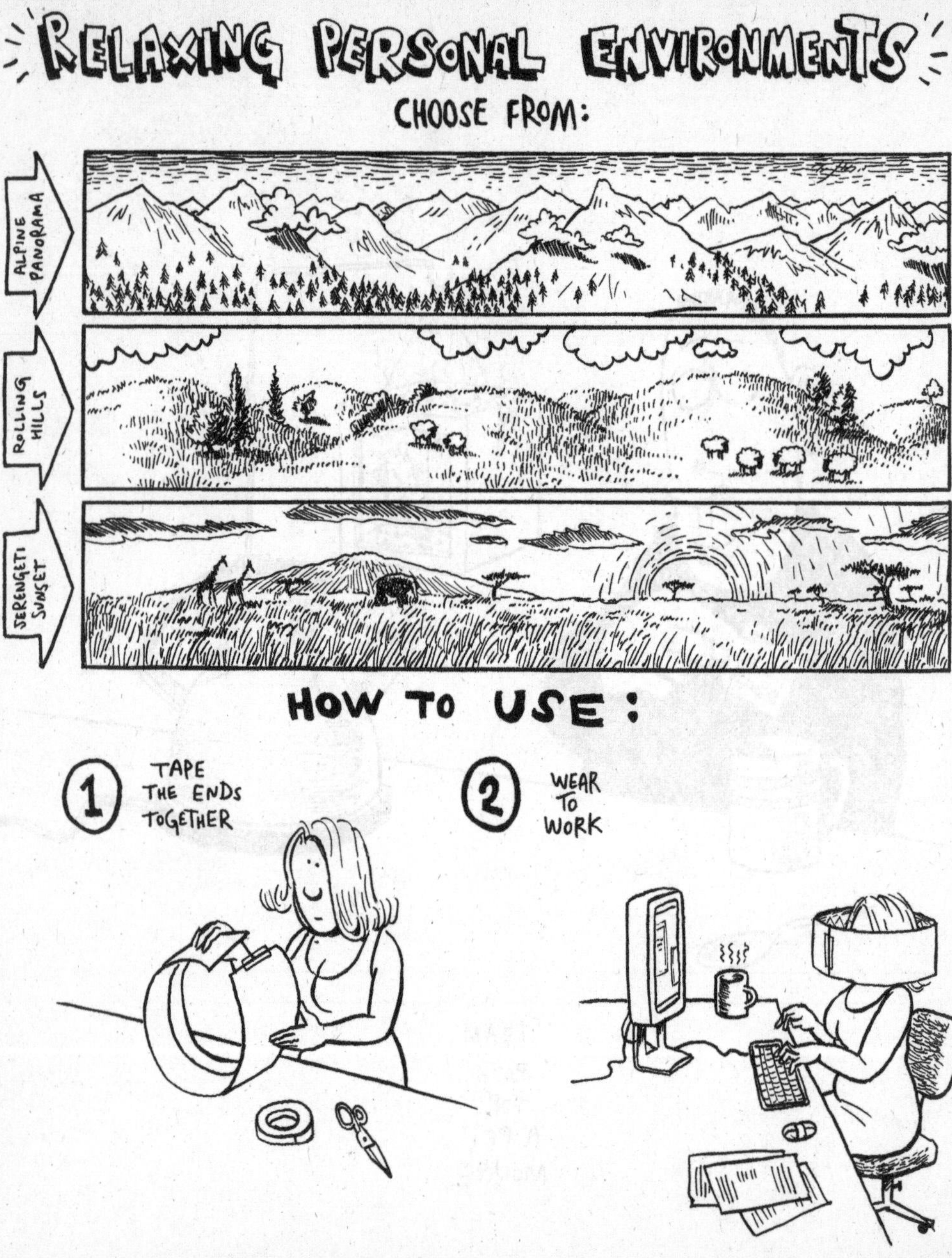
RELAXING PERSONAL ENVIRONMENTS
CHOOSE FROM:
ALPINE PANORAMA
ROLLING HILLS
SERENGETI SUNSET
HOW TO USE:
1 TAPE THE ENDS TOGETHER
2 WEAR TO WORK

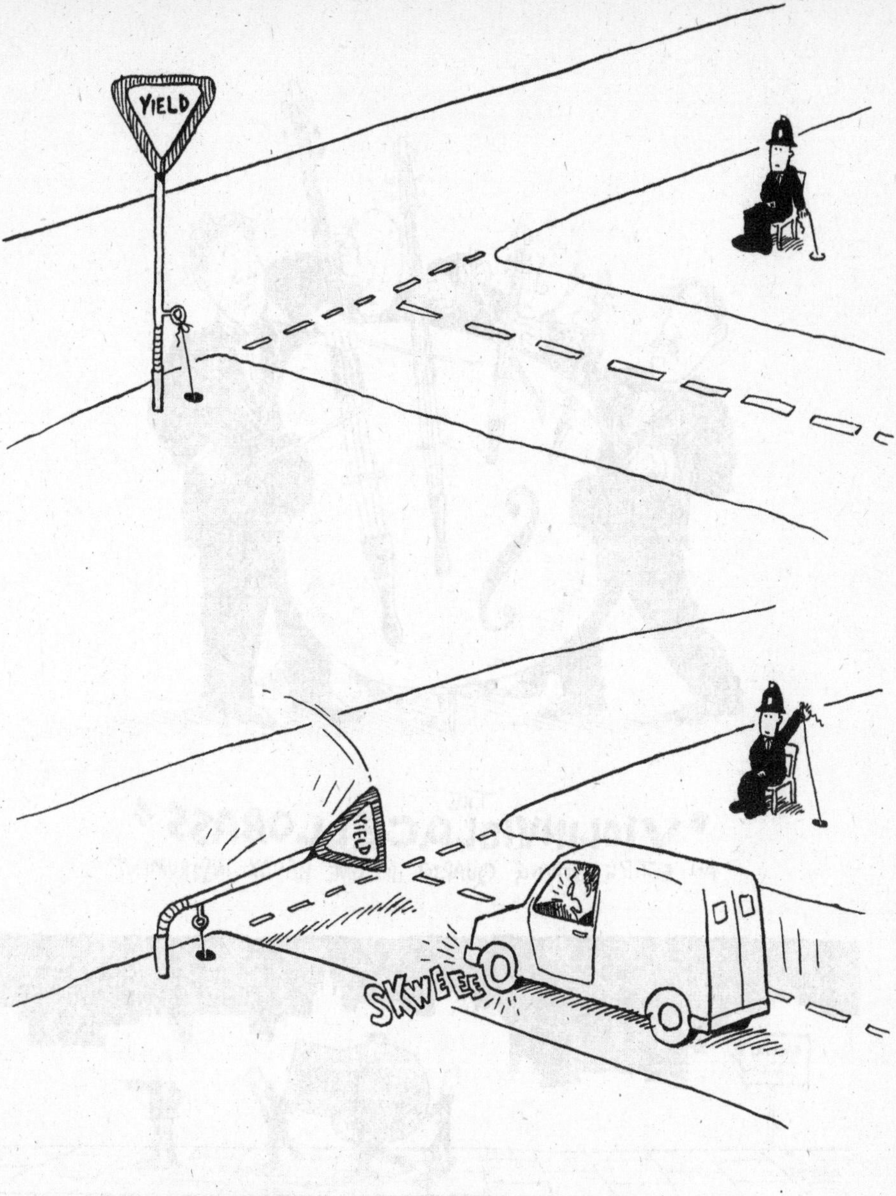
YIELD
YIELD
SKWEEE

ENFORCING "YIELD" SIGNS

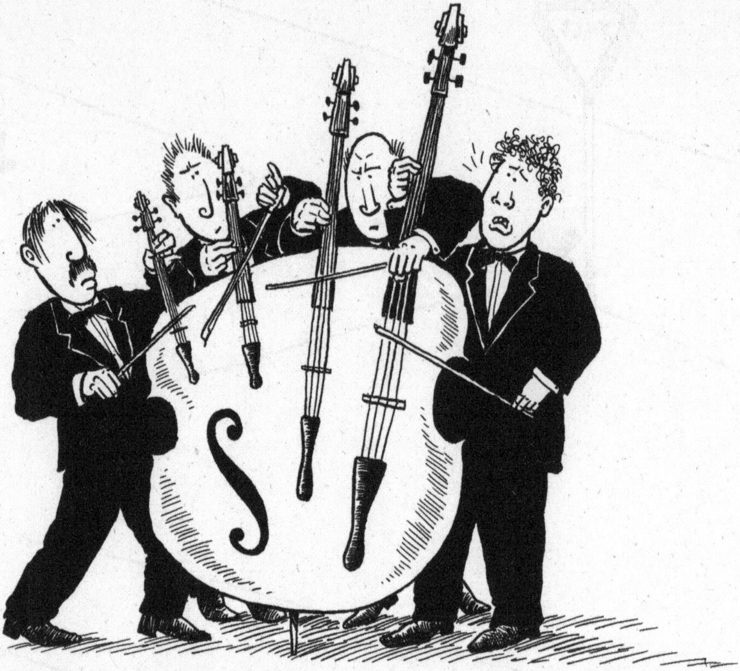

THE "VIOLINVIOLACELLOBASS"

AN ENTIRE STRING QUARTET IN ONE HANDY INSTRUMENT

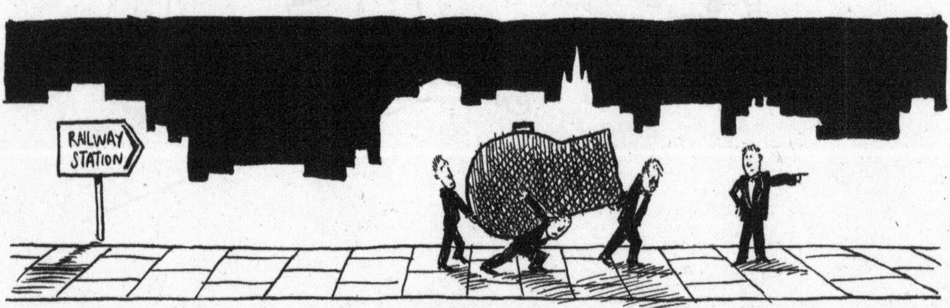
RAILWAY STATION

baby transport

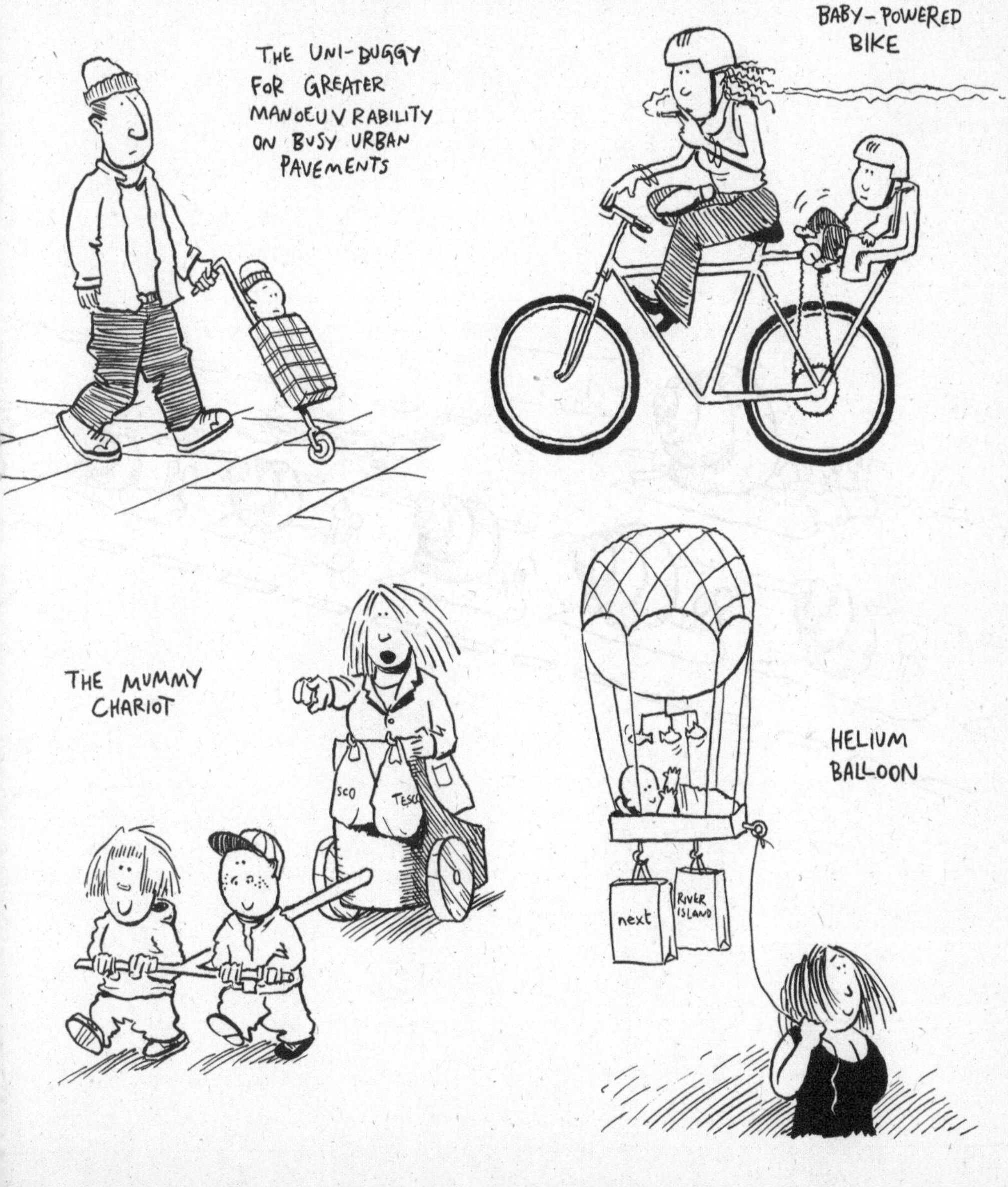
THE UNI-BUGGY FOR GREATER MANOEUVRABILITY ON BUSY URBAN PAVEMENTS
BABY-POWERED BIKE
THE MUMMY CHARIOT
SCO
TESCO
HELIUM BALLOON
next
RIVER ISLAND

SHELL-POOLING LANES FOR SNAILS

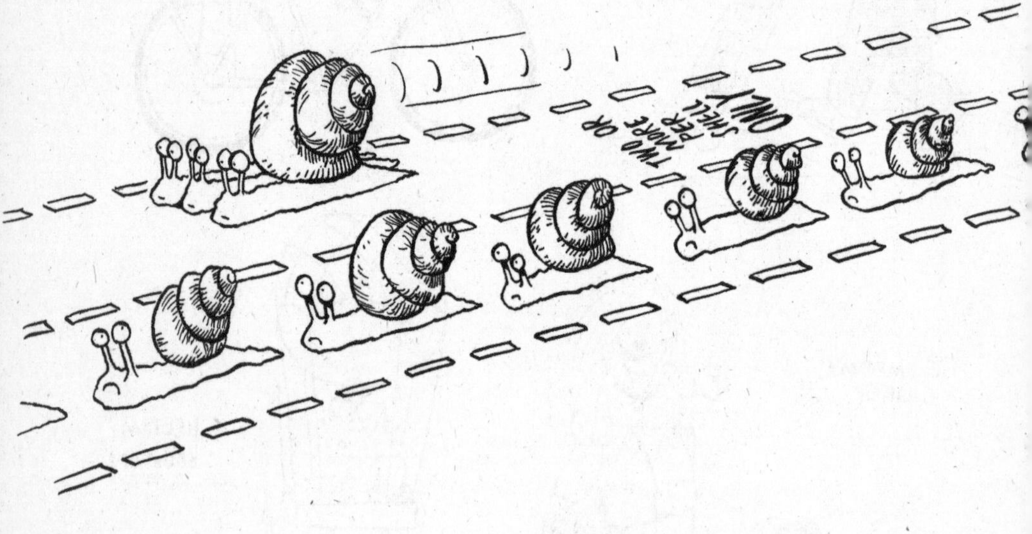

TWO OR MORE PER SHELL ONLY

BUSINESS CLASS EXECUTIONS
FOR LAW-BREAKING C.E.O.s

'CADDY TROUSERS' FOR GOLFERS

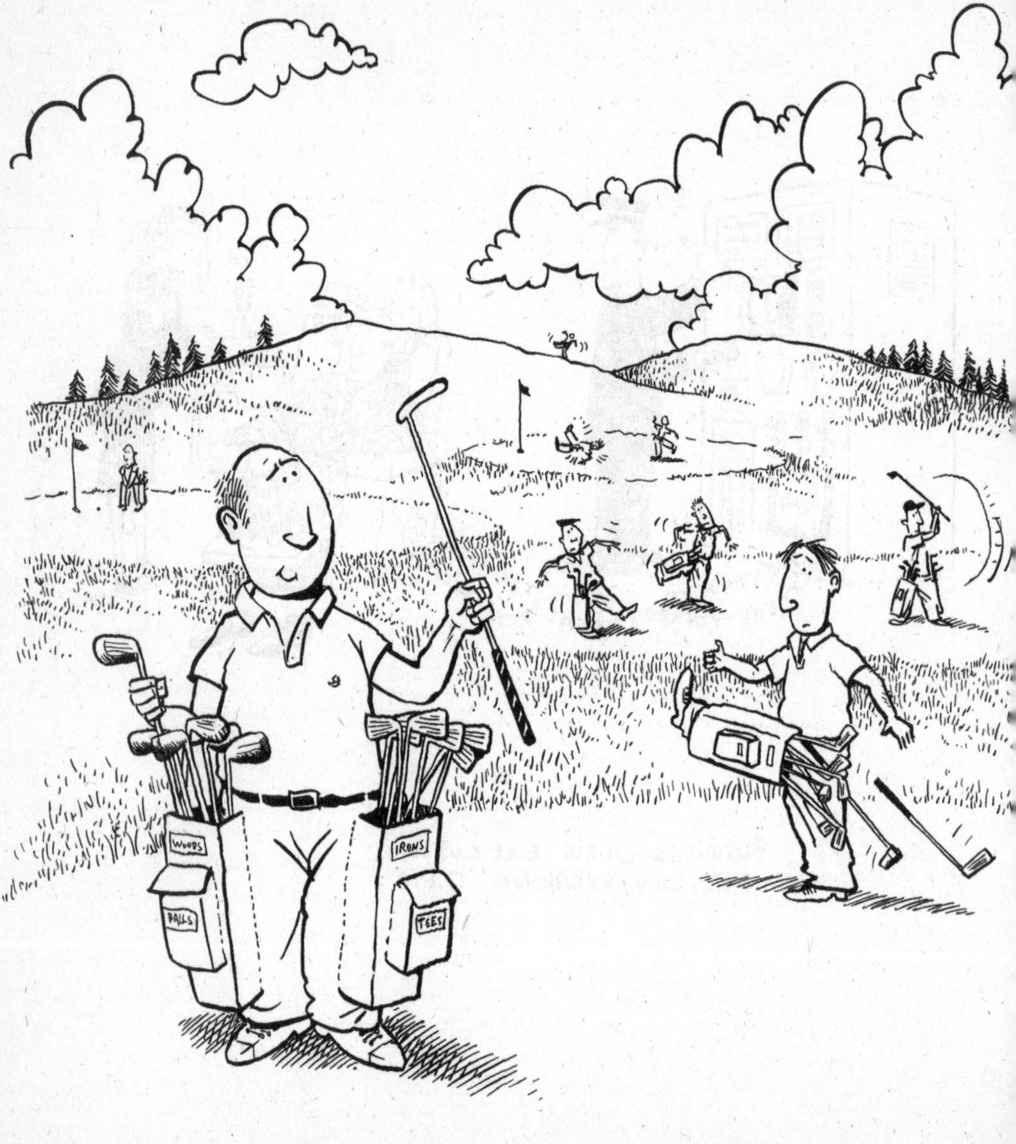
WOODS
IRONS
BALLS
TEES

HALLOWEEN FUN

NOVELTY HALLOWEEN KEBAB MEAT

WITH EMBEDDED
PLASTIC HUMAN
SKULLS AND
PELVISES

PUMPKIN LASER LANTERN

EMITS A WELCOMING ORANGE
GLOW WHICH BURNS THROUGH
TRICK-OR-TREATERS IN ⅛
OF A SECOND

'SCREAM' - THEMED
URINALS

URBAN OVERCROWDING SOLVED:

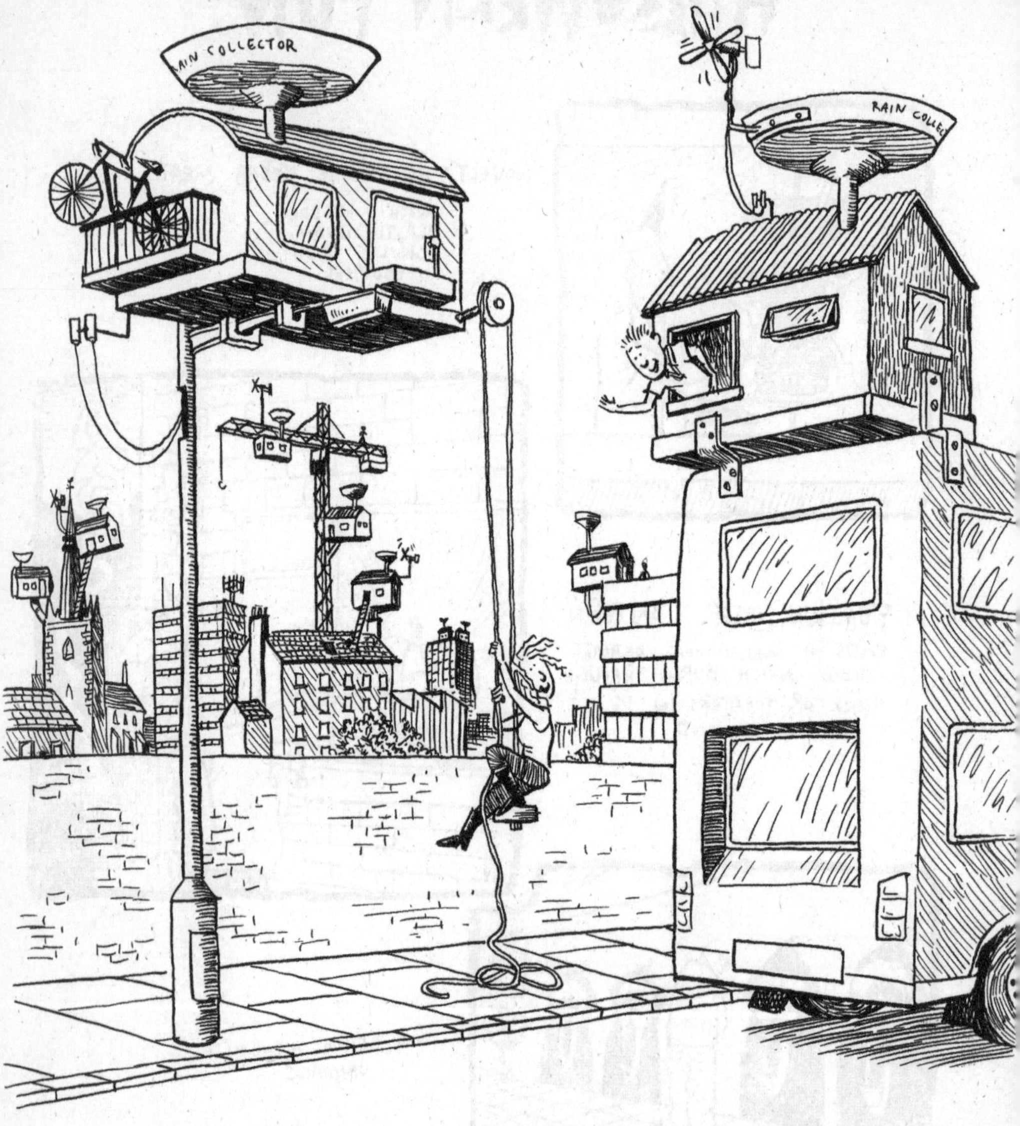
RAIN COLLECTOR
RAIN COLLEC

CLIP-ON MINI-HOMES FOR YOUNG PROFESSIONALS

100% GUARANTEED WEIGHT LOSS METHOD

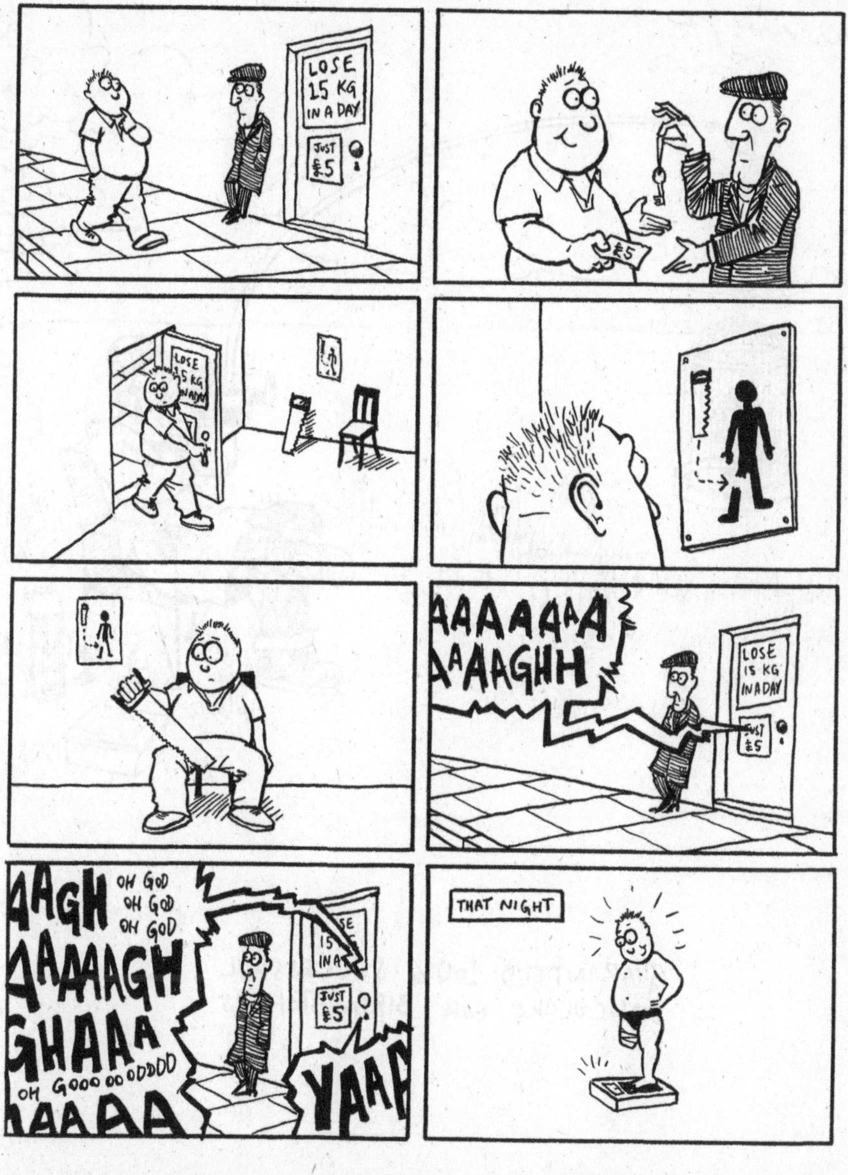
LOSE 15 KG IN A DAY
JUST £5
£5
LOSE 15 KG IN A DAY
AAAAAAA AAAAGHH
LOSE 15 KG IN A DAY
JUST £5
AAGH
OH GOD
OH GOD
OH GOD
AAAAAGH
GHAAA
OH GOOO OO ODDDD
AAAA
JUST £5
YAAR
THAT NIGHT

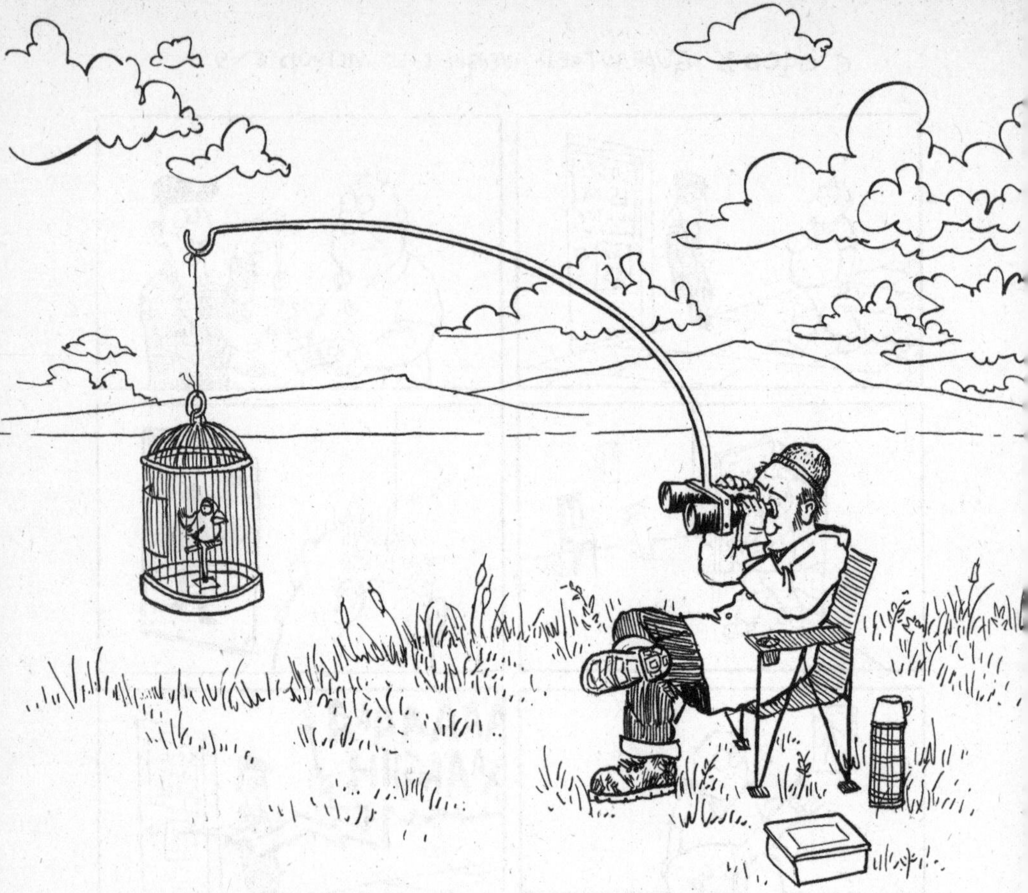

GUARANTEED 100% SUCCESSFUL
BINOCULARS FOR BIRDWATCHERS

OUTDOOR SMOKING TERRACE FOR THE A380 AIRBUS

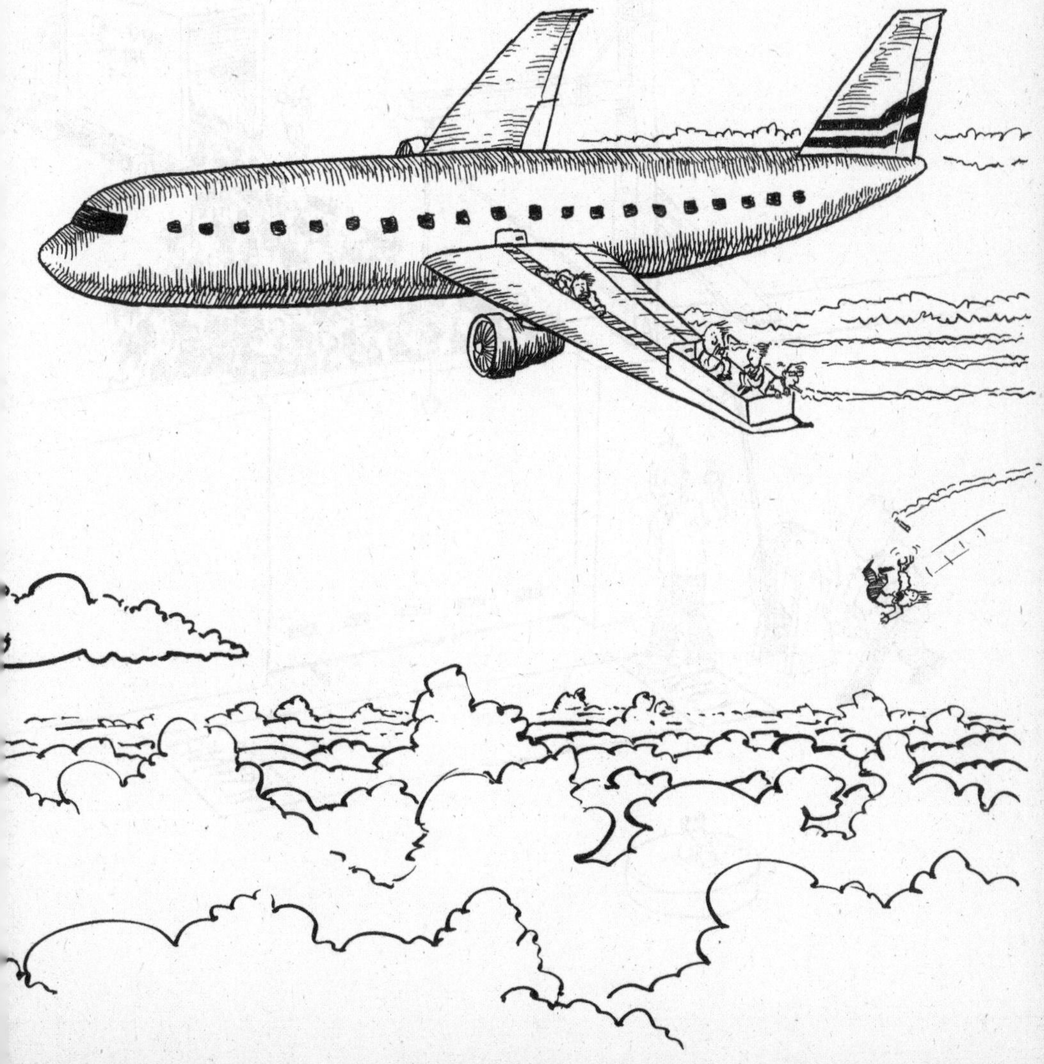

APPARATUS FOR MAKING UNLUCKY PEOPLE MORE LUCKY

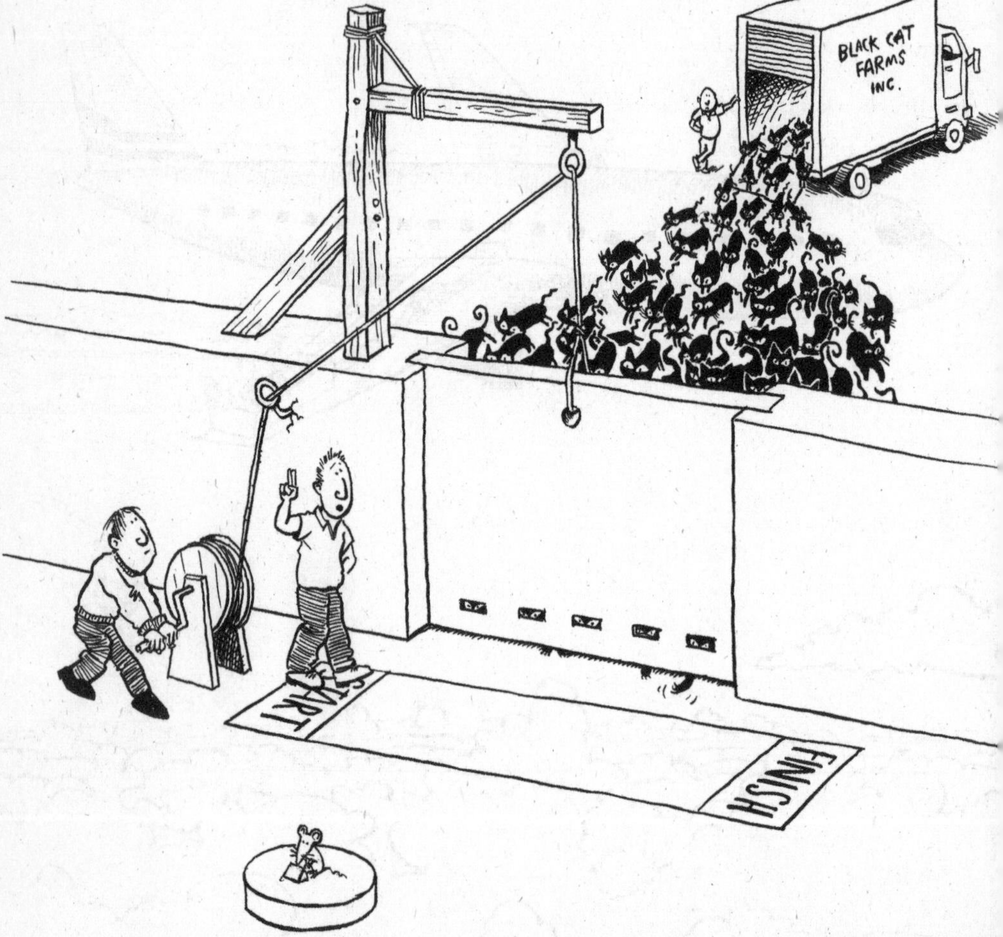
BLACK CAT FARMS INC.
START
FINISH

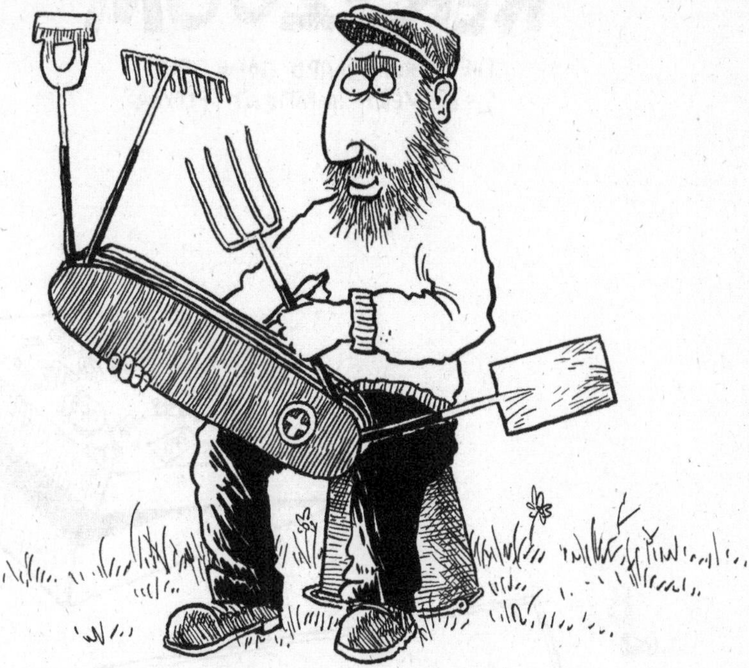

SWISS ARMY GARDEN TOOL

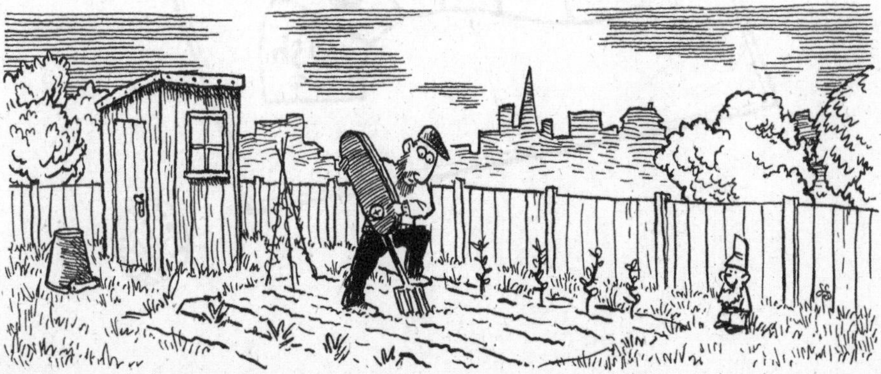

KER-ZOOM

THE NEW BOARD GAME FOR
2-6 VERY IMPATIENT PLAYERS

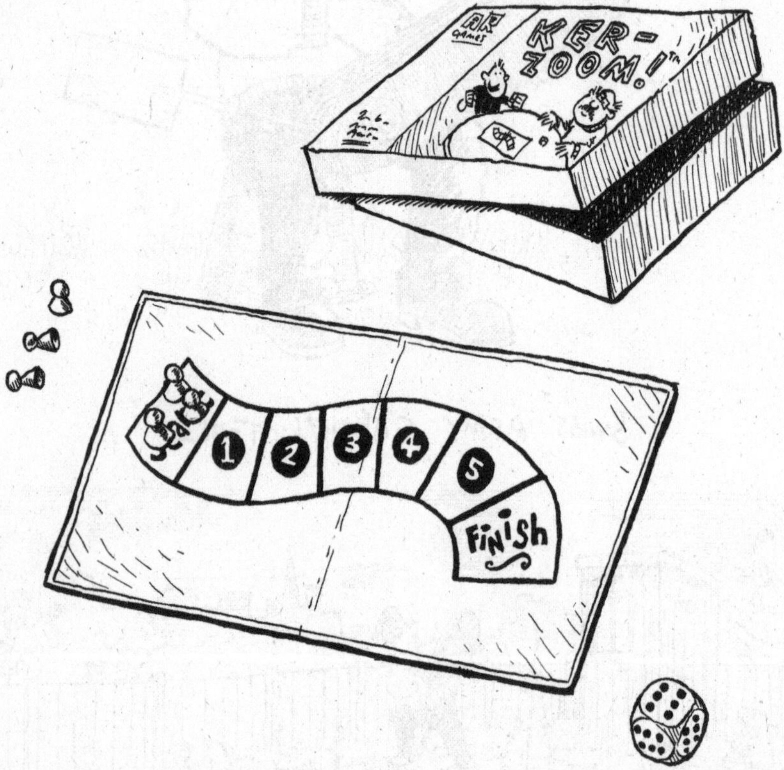
KER-ZOOM!™
1
2
3
4
5
FINISH

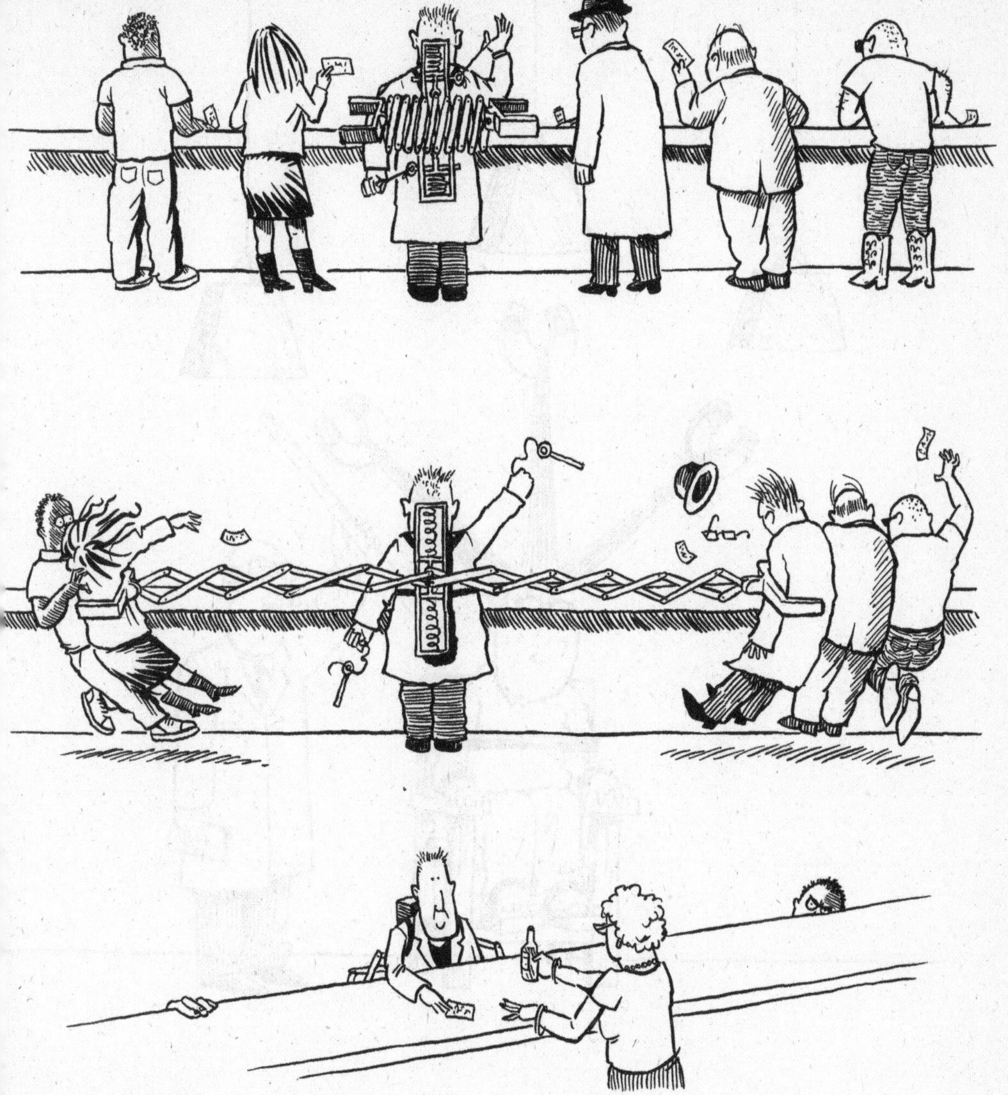

DEVICE FOR GETTING SERVED FIRST AT THE BAR

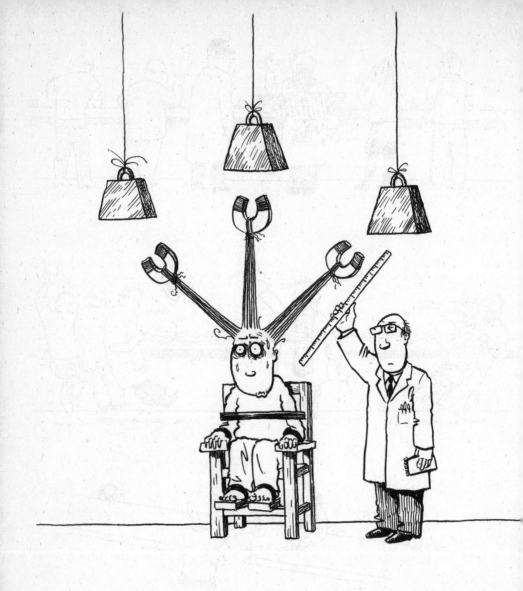

CHEAP TECHNIQUE FOR HAIR EXTENSIONS

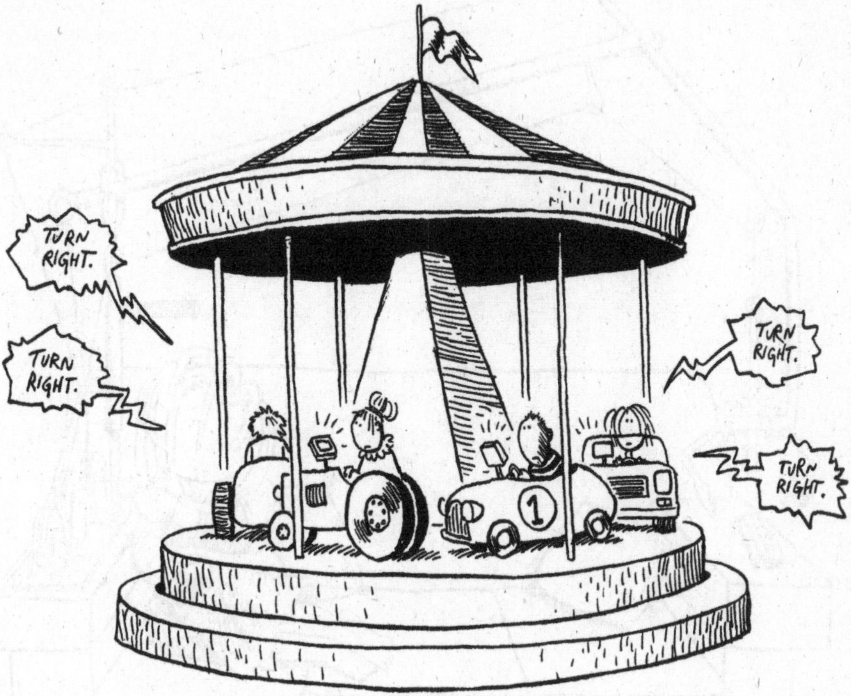
TURN RIGHT.
TURN RIGHT.
TURN RIGHT.
TURN RIGHT.

JUNIOR GPS

FOR LITTLE KID'S RIDES

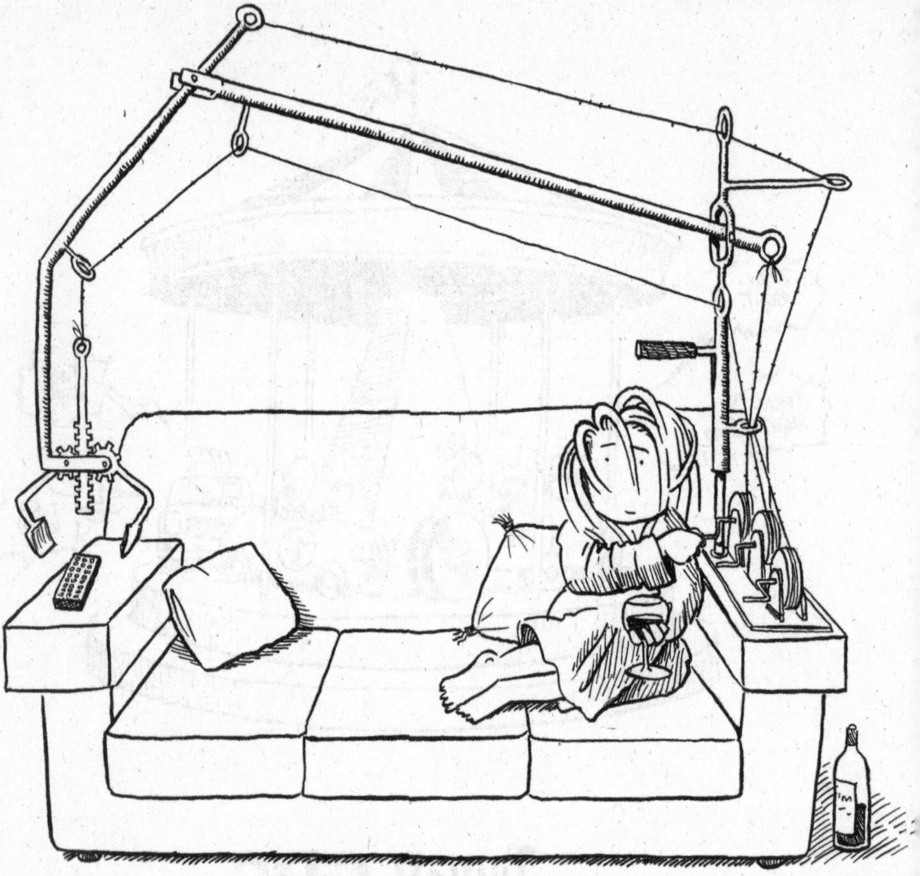

MACHINE FOR GETTING THE REMOTE CONTROL
FROM THE OTHER END OF THE SOFA

"SKATEBOARD-HOSTILE" PARK FURNITURE

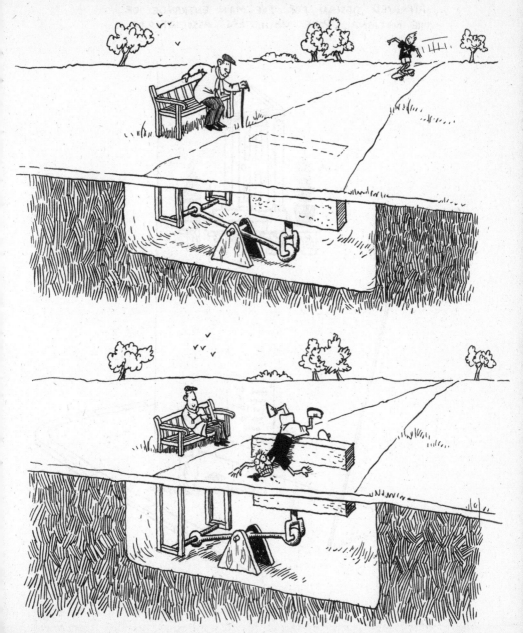

APPROVED DESIGN FOR THE MAIN ENTRANCE OF THE NATIONAL POLE VAULTERS' ASSOCIATION

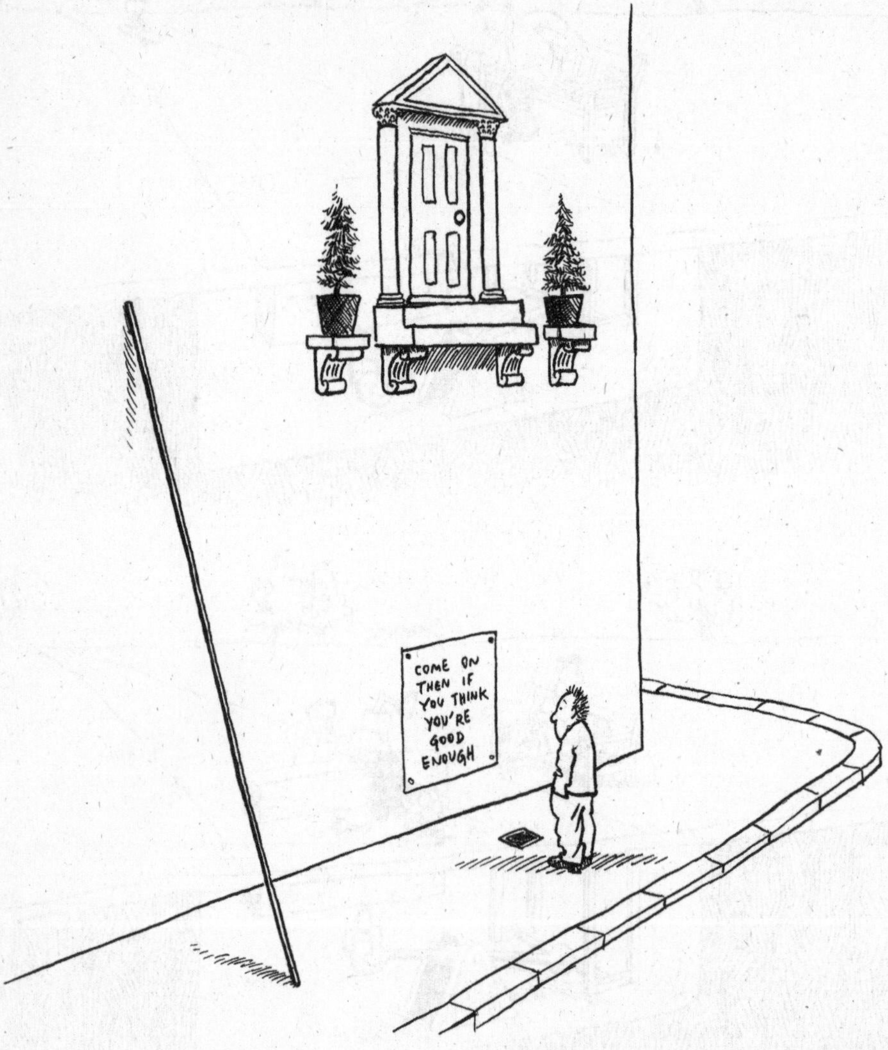
COME ON THEN IF YOU THINK YOU'RE GOOD ENOUGH

folk tales

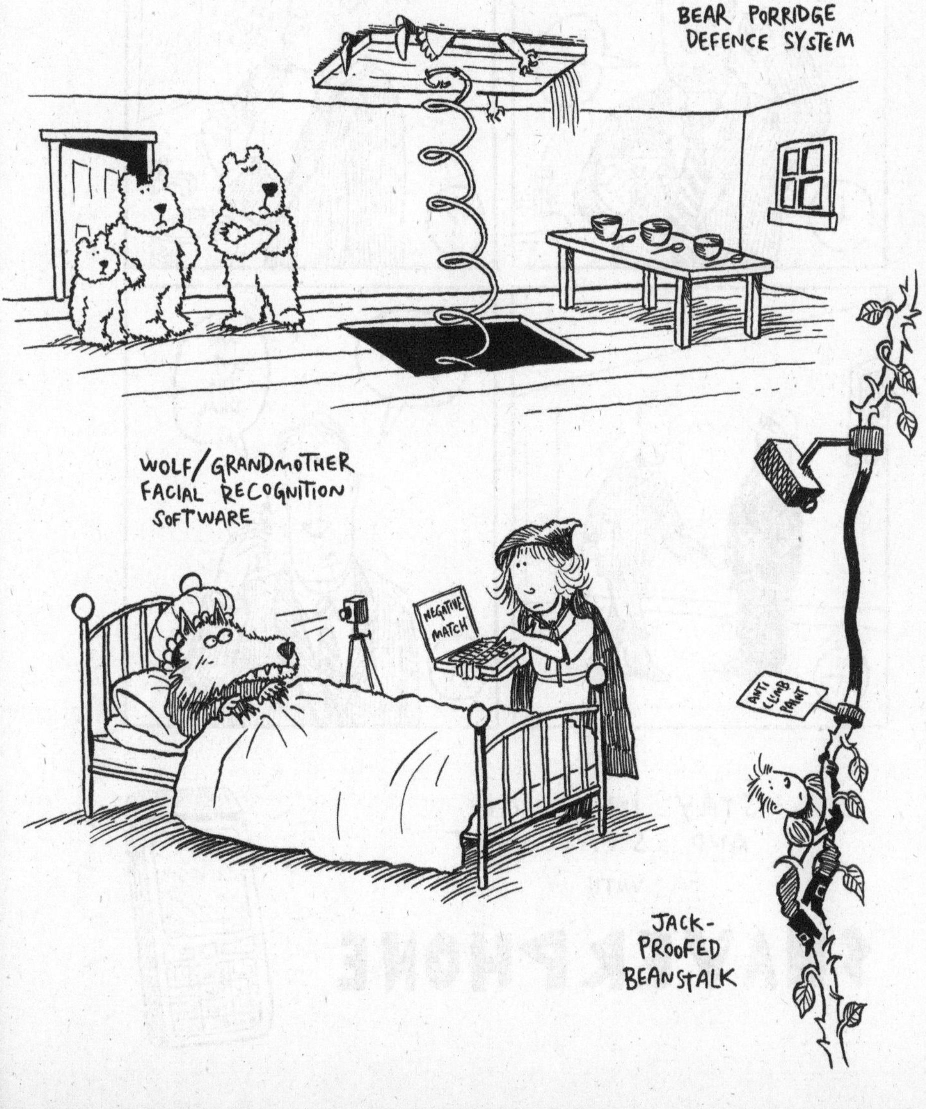
BEAR PORRIDGE
DEFENCE SYSTEM
WOLF/GRANDMOTHER
FACIAL RECOGNITION
SOFTWARE
NEGATIVE
MATCH
ANTI
CLIMB
PAINT
JACK-
PROOFED
BEANSTALK

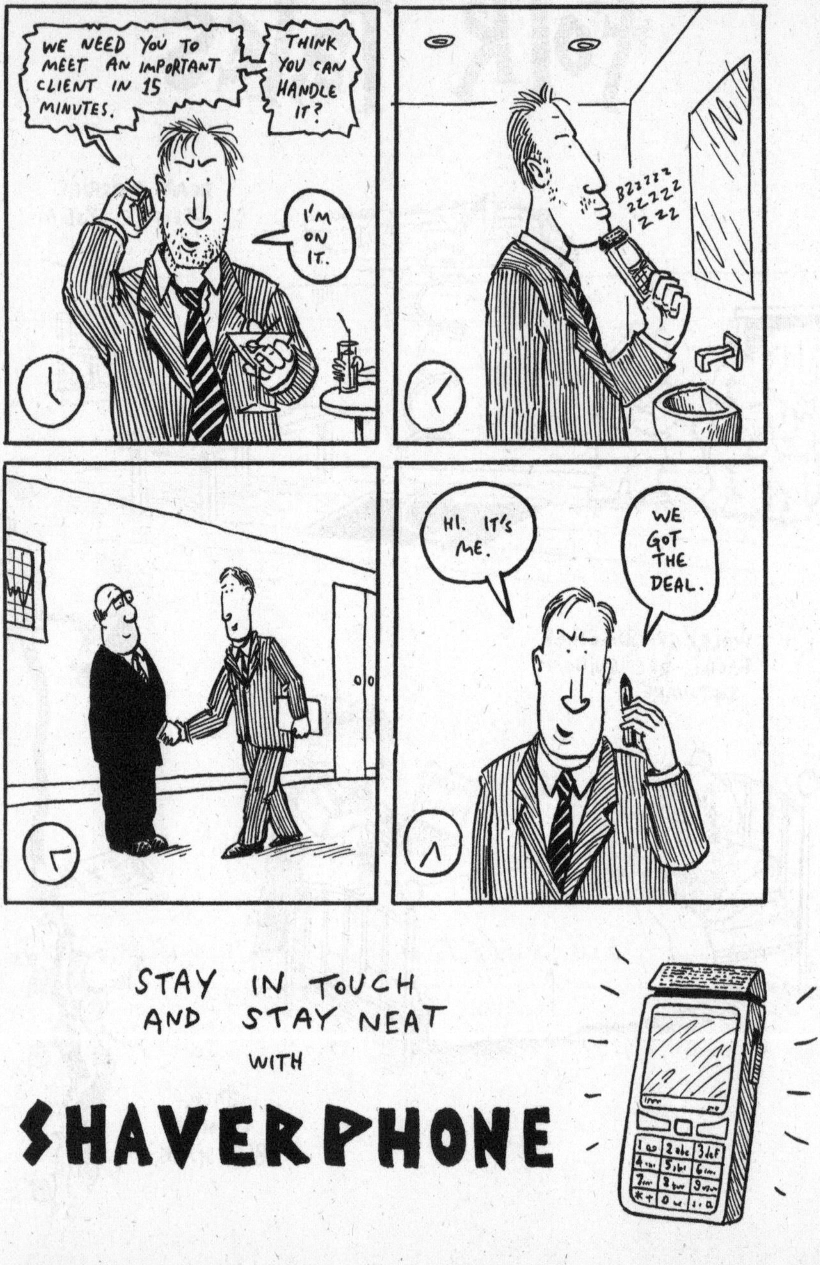

WE NEED YOU TO MEET AN IMPORTANT CLIENT IN 15 MINUTES.
THINK YOU CAN HANDLE IT?
I'M ON IT.
BZZZZZ ZZZZZ ZZZZ
HI. IT'S ME.
WE GOT THE DEAL.
STAY IN TOUCH AND STAY NEAT
WITH
SHAVERPHONE

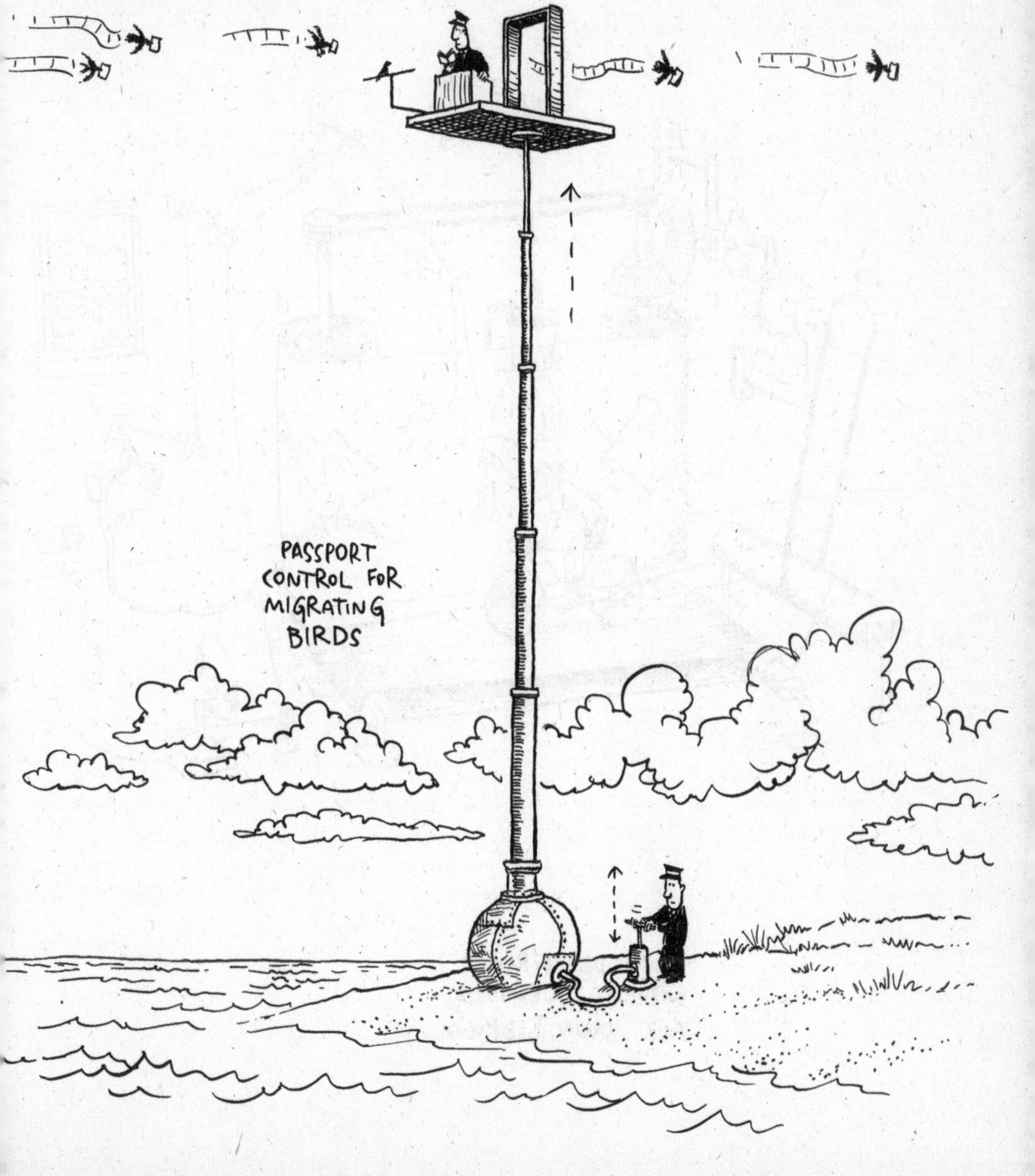
PASSPORT CONTROL FOR MIGRATING BIRDS

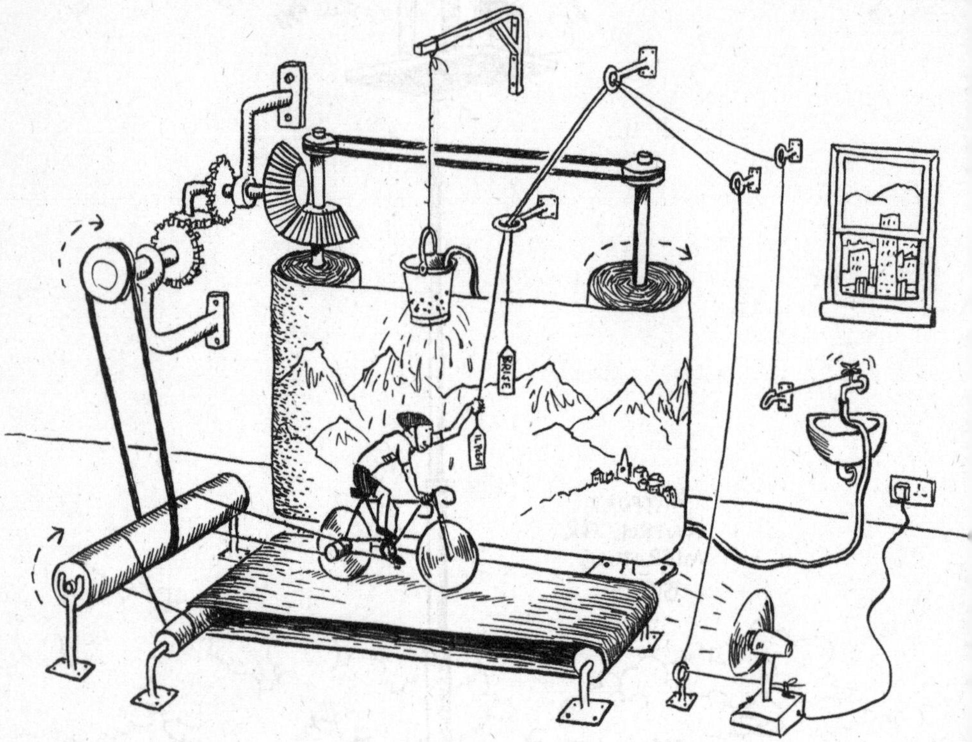
BRISE
IL PLEUT

TOUR DE FRANCE
WITHOUT LEAVING
YOUR OWN BEDROOM

"SLIP-ON" IRONS FOR HANDS-FREE DE-WRINKLING

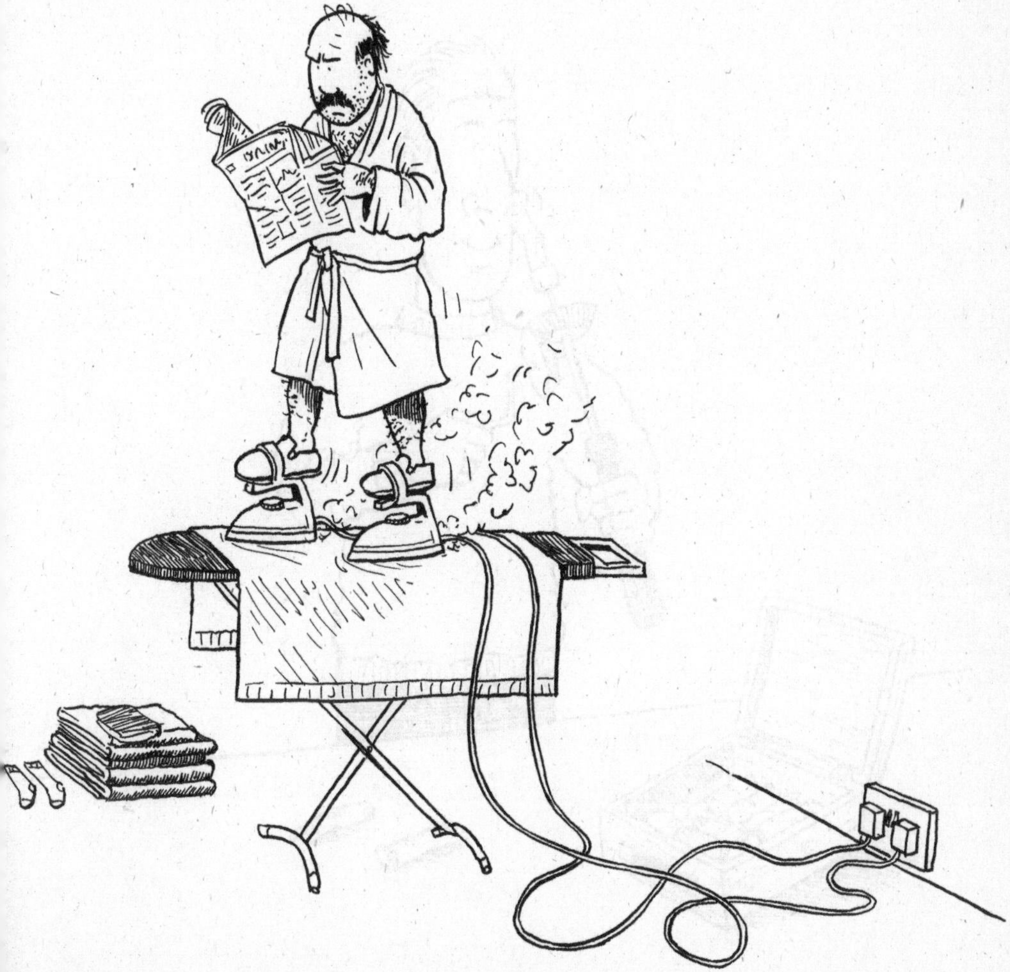

ROTARY NOSE PICKER

- GOES CLOCKWISE OR COUNTERCLOCKWISE
- COMES WITH 30-PIECE SET OF DIFFERENT SIZED INDEX FINGERS

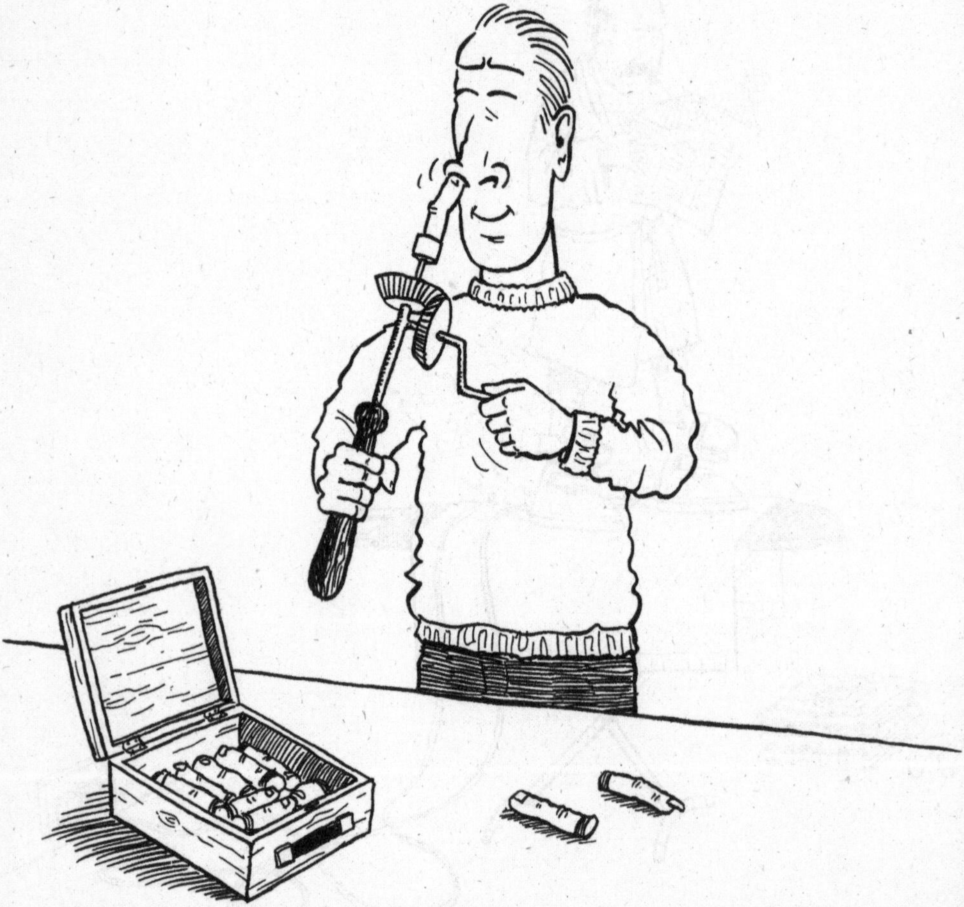

HUSBAND PUB SESSION TERMINATION SYSTEM

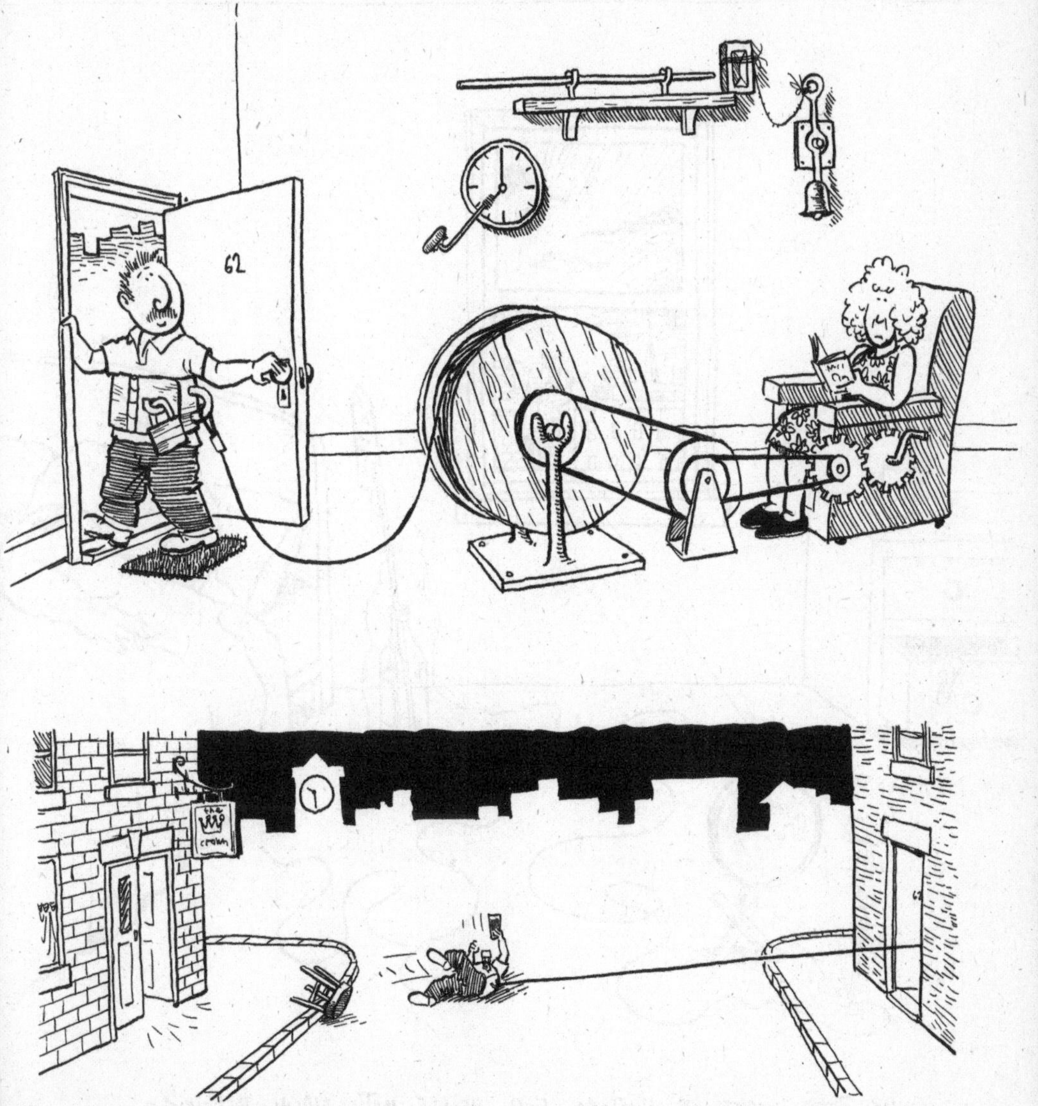
62

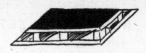

GUARANTEED WAKE UP SYSTEM FOR PEOPLE WITH NASAL PIERCINGS

CAMPERVAN SKATEBOARD

GREEN POWER

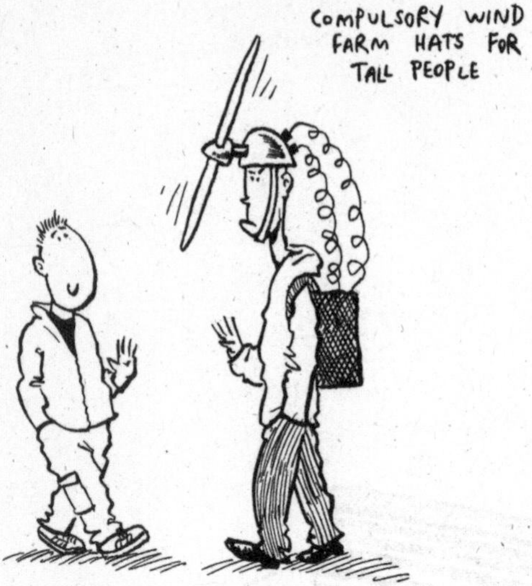
COMPULSORY WIND FARM HATS FOR TALL PEOPLE

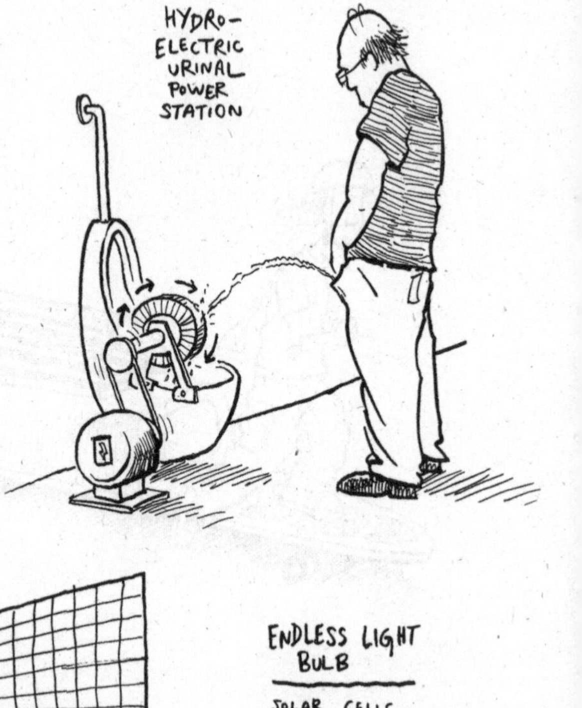
HYDRO-ELECTRIC URINAL POWER STATION

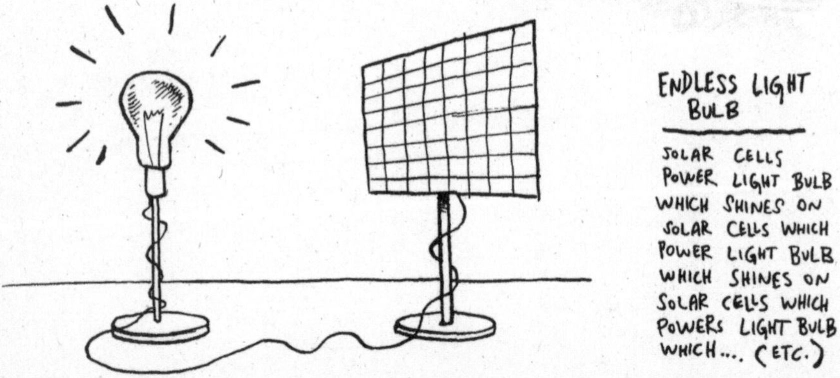
ENDLESS LIGHT BULB
SOLAR CELLS POWER LIGHT BULB WHICH SHINES ON SOLAR CELLS WHICH POWER LIGHT BULB WHICH SHINES ON SOLAR CELLS WHICH POWERS LIGHT BULB WHICH.... (ETC.)

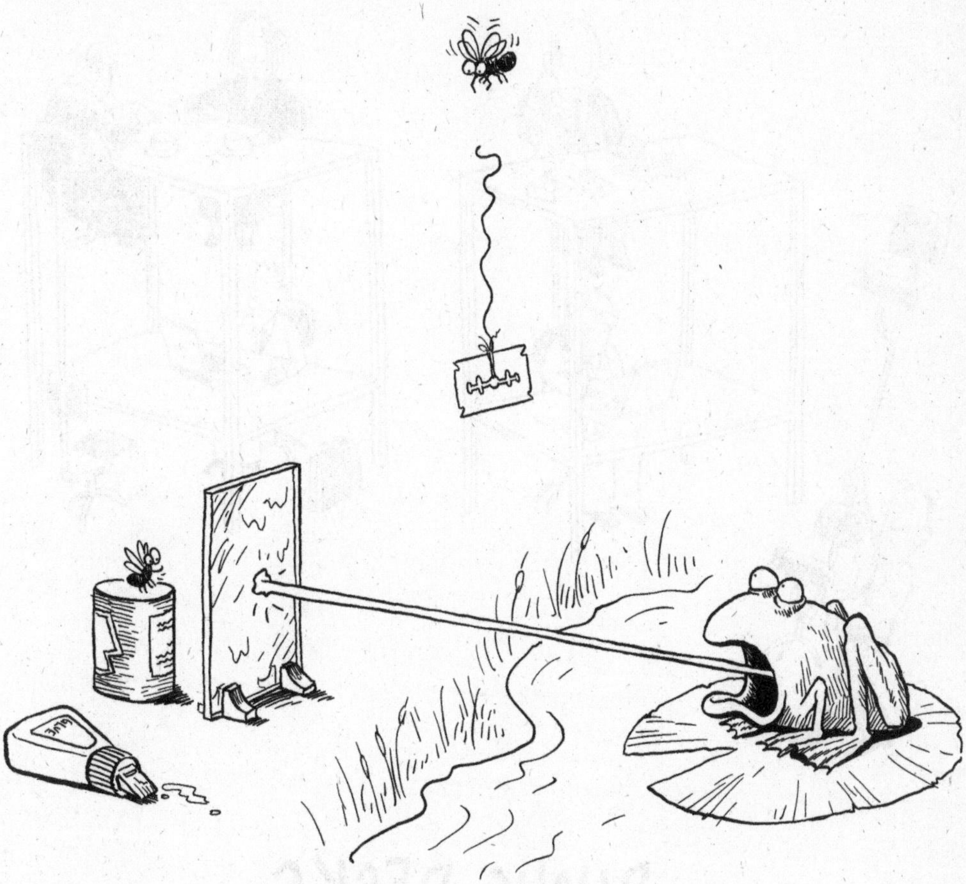

FROG NEUTRALISATION SYSTEM
FOR POND-DWELLING FLIES

BUNK DESKS

SAVING SPACE IN THE MODERN OFFICE

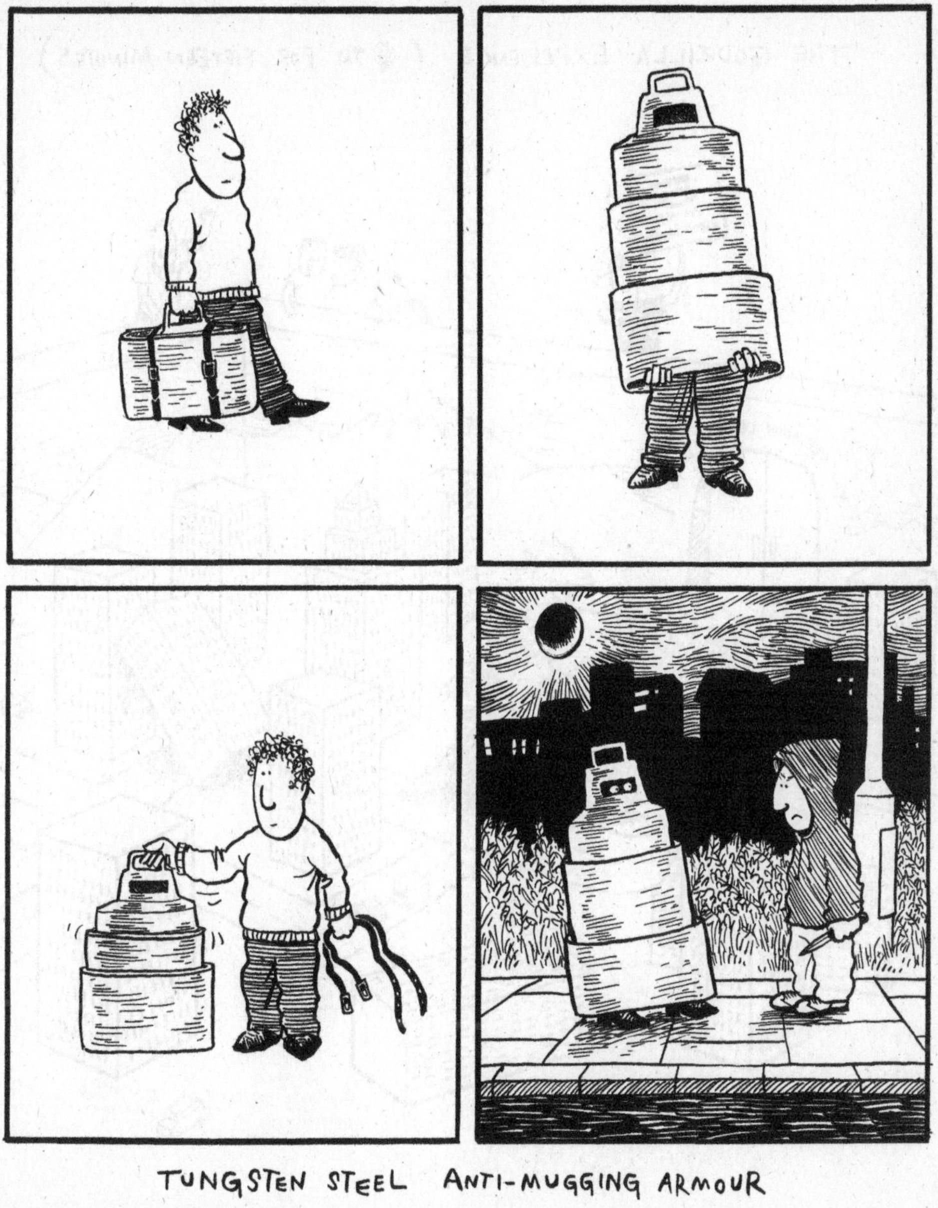

TUNGSTEN STEEL ANTI-MUGGING ARMOUR

THE GODZILLA EXPERIENCE ($70 FOR FIFTEEN MINUTES)

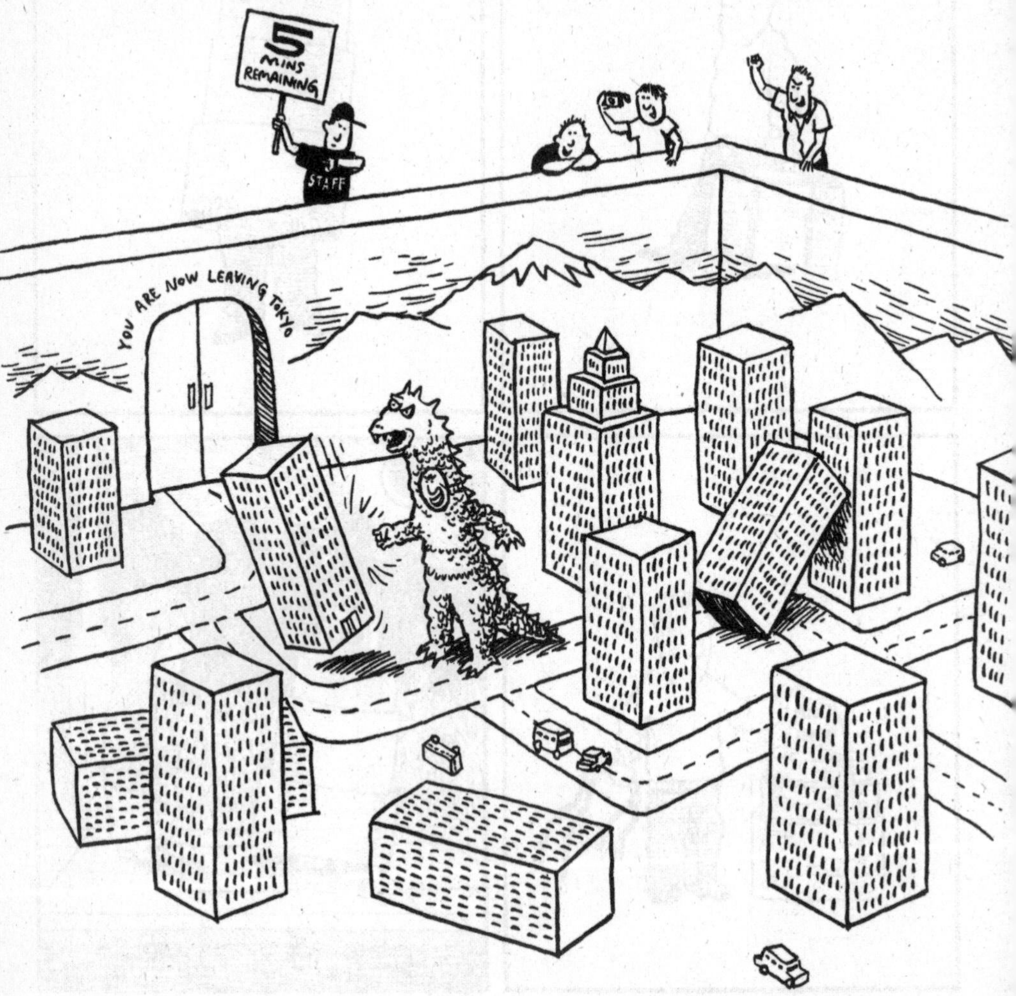
5
MINS
REMAINING
STAFF
YOU ARE NOW LEAVING TOKYO

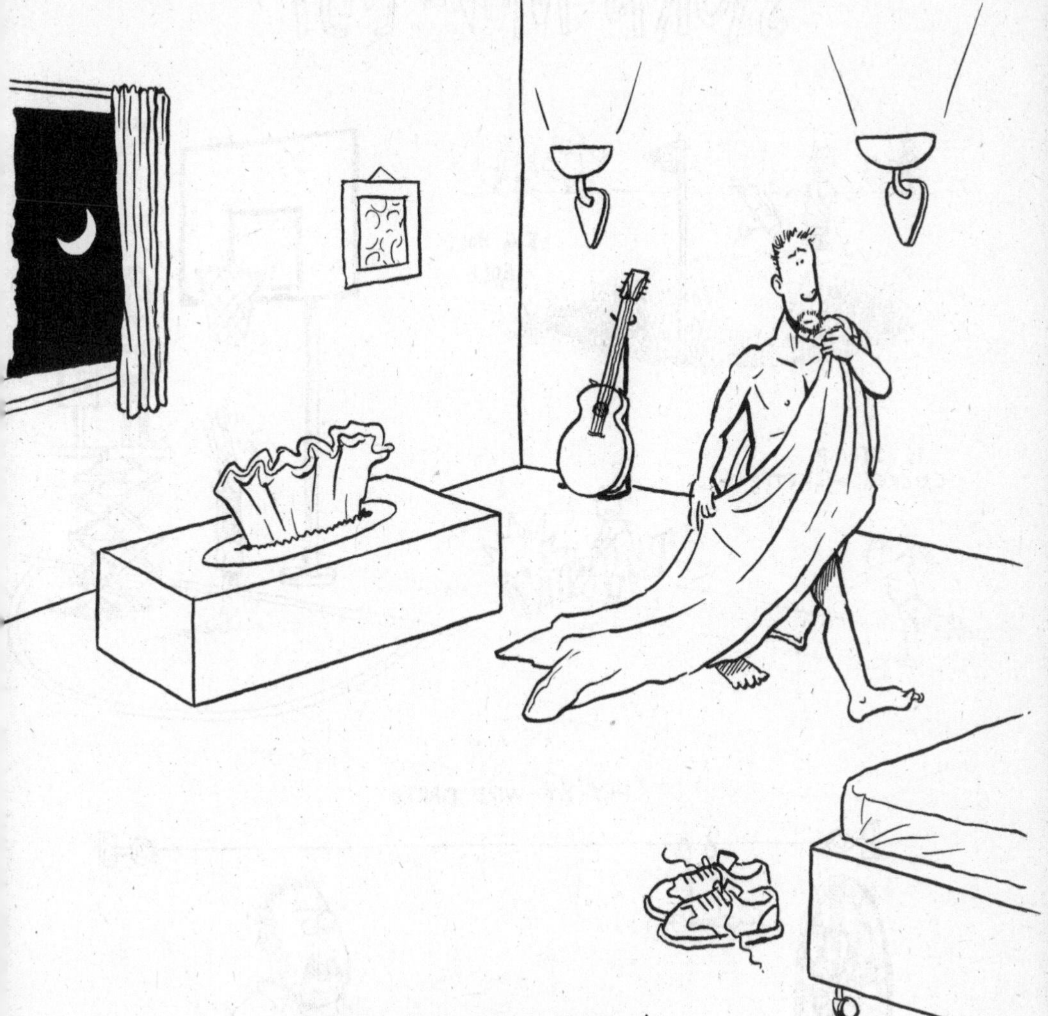

BOX OF 100 'MAN-SIZE'
DISPOSABLE DUVETS

SPORTS MADE EASY

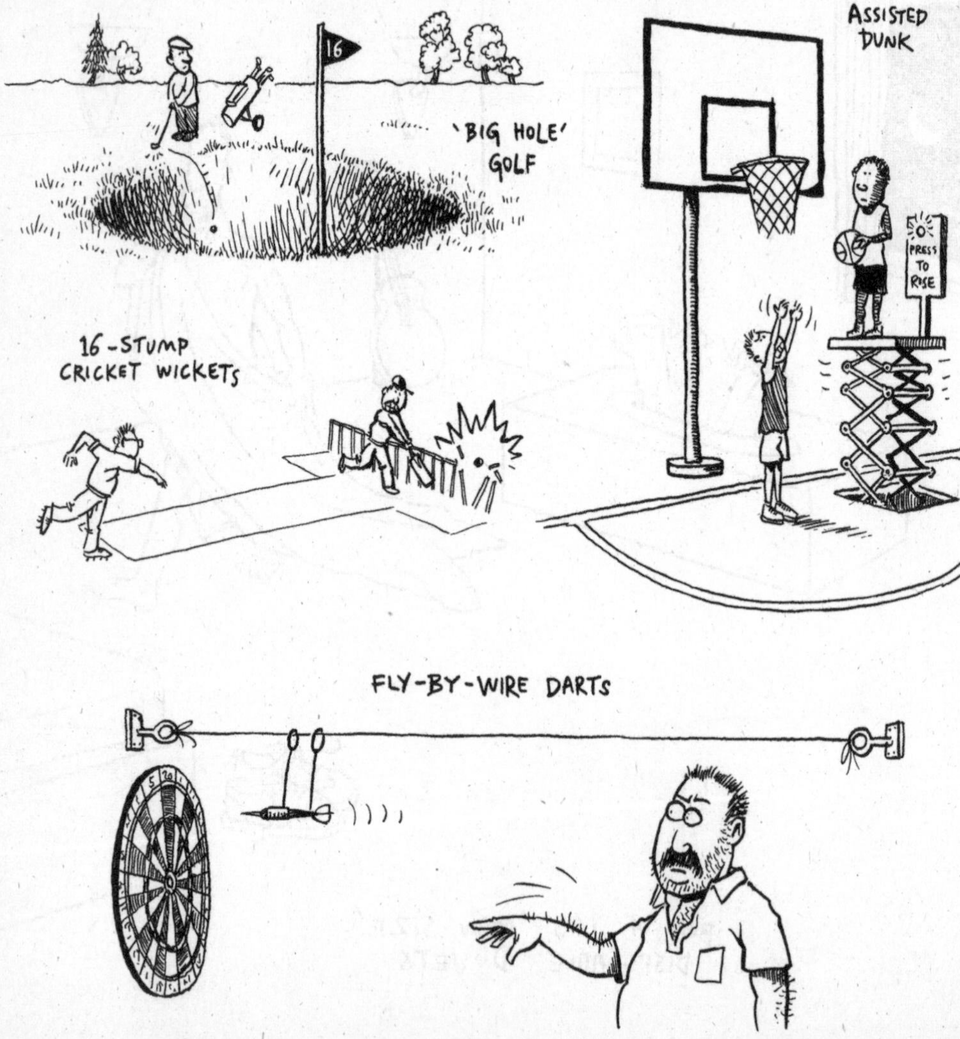
16
'BIG HOLE' GOLF
ASSISTED DUNK
PRESS TO RISE
16-STUMP CRICKET WICKETS
FLY-BY-WIRE DARTS

INSTANT CYCLEPATH

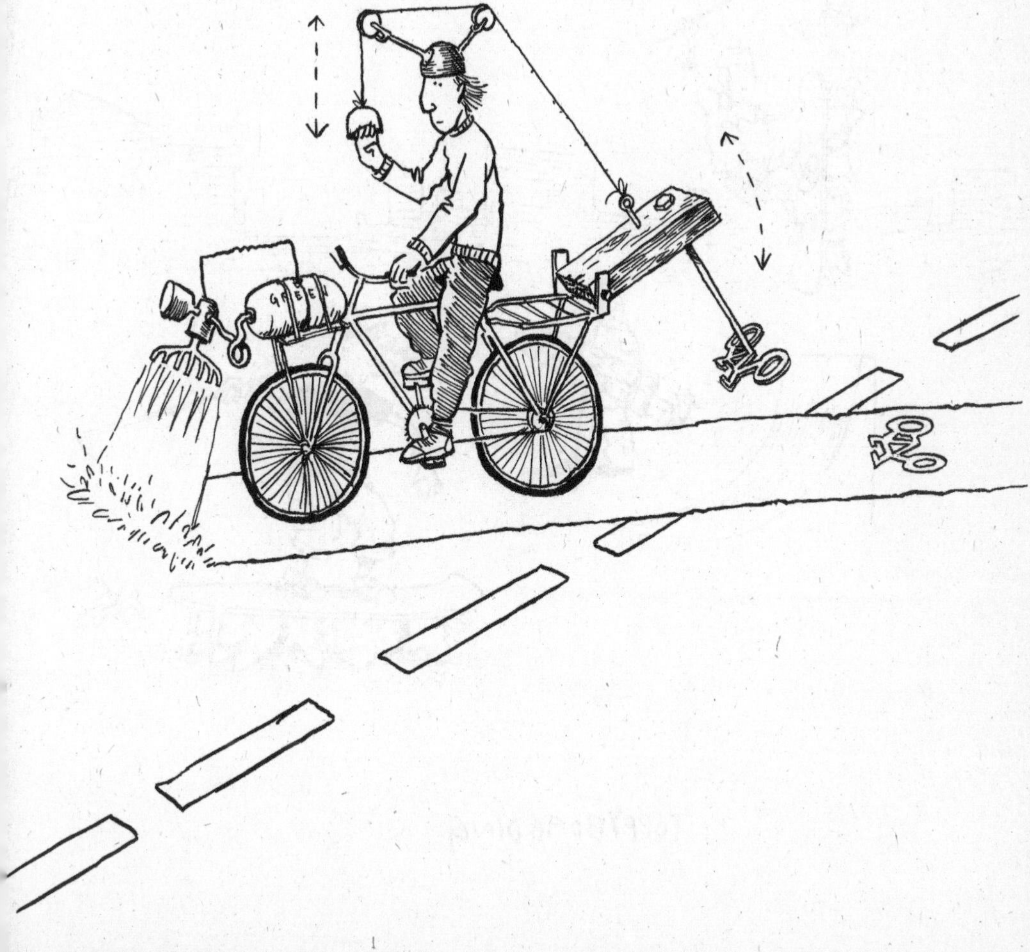
GREEN

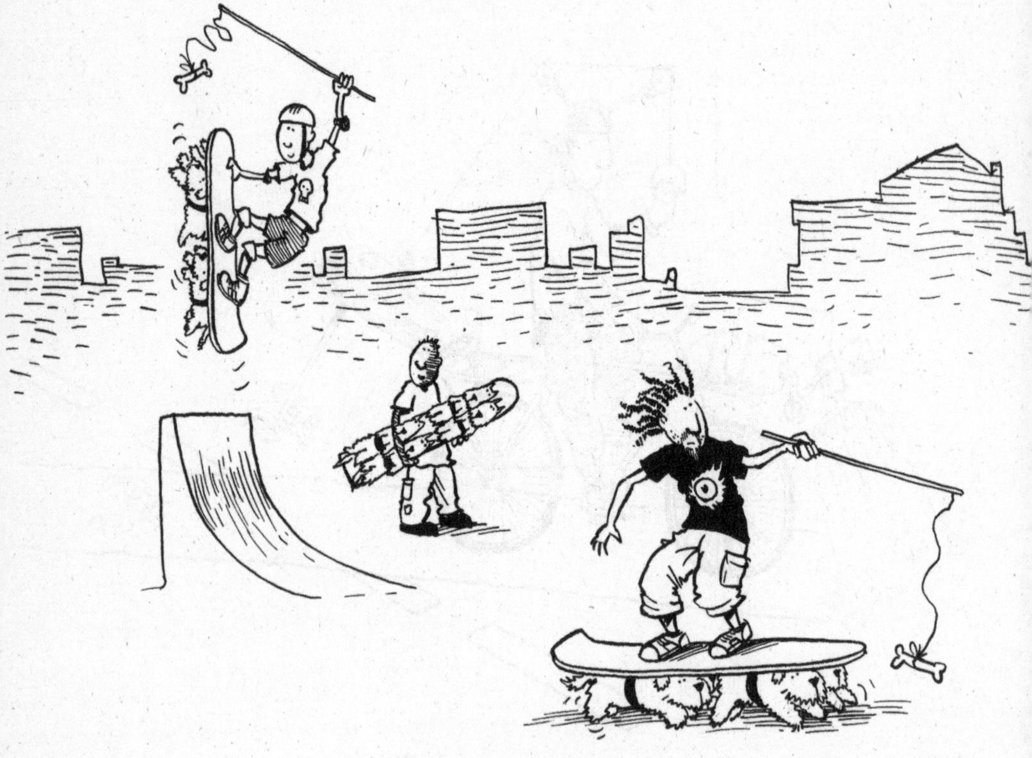

PUPPYBOARDING

SOLITAIRE BOXING

More Humor from the
"Wonderfully Deviant"* Andy Riley